First World War
and Army of Occupation
War Diary
France, Belgium and Germany

62 DIVISION
Divisional Troops
Royal Army Medical Corps
2/3 West Riding Field Ambulance
10 January 1917 - 31 August 1919

WO95/3078/3

Published by

The Naval & Military Press Ltd

Unit 10 Ridgewood Industrial Park,

Uckfield, East Sussex,

TN22 5QE England

Tel: +44 (0) 1825 749494

www.naval-military-press.com

www.nmarchive.com

This diary has been reprinted in facsimile from the original. Any imperfections are inevitably reproduced and the quality may fall short of modern type and cartographic standards.

© **Crown Copyright**
Images reproduced by permission of The National Archives, London, England, 2015.

Contents

Document type	Place/Title	Date From	Date To
Heading	WO95/3078/3		
Heading	62nd Division 2-3rd (W. R.) Fld Ambulance Jan 1917-1919 Aug		
Heading	War Diary of 2/3rd West Riding Field Ambulance From 10th Jany 1917 To 31st Jany 1917 Volume I		
War Diary	Wellingboro	10/01/1917	10/01/1917
War Diary	La. Havre	12/01/1917	13/01/1917
War Diary	Ransart	14/01/1917	22/01/1917
War Diary	Beauval	23/01/1917	23/01/1917
War Diary	Louvencourt	23/01/1917	31/01/1917
Heading	War Diary of 2/3rd W.R. Field Ambulance From 1st Feb 1917 To 28th Feb 1917 Volume II		
War Diary	Lowvencourt	03/02/1917	11/02/1917
War Diary	Bus-Le-Artois	16/02/1917	16/02/1917
War Diary	Forceville	23/02/1917	23/02/1917
Heading	War Diary of 2/3rd W.R. Field Ambulance From 1st March 1917 To 31st March 1917 Volume 3		
War Diary	Forceville	01/03/1917	29/03/1917
Diagram etc	2/3rd W.R. Field Ambulance		
Heading	62nd Div 2/3rd West Riding F.A.		
Heading	War Diary of 2/3rd W.R. Field Ambulance From 1st April 1917 To 30th April 1917 Volume IV		
War Diary	Forceville	03/04/1917	12/04/1917
War Diary	Bihucourt	14/04/1917	14/04/1917
War Diary	Achiet-Le-Grand	14/04/1917	30/04/1917
Operation(al) Order(s)	Operation Order R.A.M.C. 2nd Division No.13	09/04/1917	09/04/1917
Heading	62nd Div 2/3rd West Riding F.A.		
Heading	War Diary of 2/3rd West Riding Field Ambulance From 1st May 1917 To 31st May 1917 Volume V		
War Diary	Achiet-Le-Grand	01/05/1917	12/05/1917
War Diary	Bucquoy	12/05/1917	16/05/1917
War Diary	Courcelles	18/05/1917	29/05/1917
War Diary	Gomiecourt	29/05/1917	30/05/1917
Heading	War Diary Of 2/3 West Riding Field Ambulance Volume VI June 1917		
War Diary	Gomiecourt	01/06/1917	24/06/1917
War Diary	Favreuil	27/06/1917	29/06/1917
Map	France		
Heading	War Diary 2/3 West Riding Field Ambulance July 1917 Volume 7		
War Diary	Favreuil	04/07/1917	31/07/1917
Heading	War Diary Of 2/3 West Riding Field Ambulance Volume VIII-August 1917		
War Diary	Favreuil	01/08/1917	31/08/1917
Heading	War Diary Of 2/3 West Riding Field Ambulance Volume IX September 1917		
War Diary	Favreuil	01/09/1917	30/09/1917
Heading	War Diary Of 2/3rd West Riding Field Ambulance October 1917 Volume X		
War Diary	Favreuil	01/10/1917	11/10/1917

War Diary	Lechelle	12/10/1917	29/10/1917
War Diary	Gomiecourt	30/10/1917	30/10/1917
War Diary	Berneville	31/10/1917	31/10/1917
Miscellaneous	Scheme Of Evacuation From Right Sector		
Heading	War Diary Of 2/3 West Riding Field Ambulance Volume XI November 1917		
War Diary	Berneville	01/11/1917	12/11/1917
War Diary	Gomiecourt	13/11/1917	13/11/1917
War Diary	Lechelle	14/11/1917	16/11/1917
War Diary	Ruyaulcourt	17/11/1917	19/11/1917
War Diary	Active Operations Map 57e	19/11/1917	23/11/1917
War Diary	Ruyaulcourt	24/11/1917	24/11/1917
War Diary	Active Operations Map 57c	25/11/1917	30/11/1917
Heading	War Diary Of 2/3 West Riding Field Ambulance 1st To 31st December 1917 Volume XII		
War Diary	Lebucquire	01/12/1917	03/12/1917
War Diary	Blaireville	04/12/1917	04/12/1917
War Diary	Duisans	05/12/1917	05/12/1917
War Diary	Bethonsart	06/12/1917	09/12/1917
War Diary	Hesdigneul	10/12/1917	18/12/1917
War Diary	Hermin	19/12/1917	31/12/1917
Heading	War Diary Of 2/3rd West Riding Field Ambulance January 1918 Volume XIII		
War Diary	Hermin	01/01/1918	08/01/1918
War Diary	Anzin St Aubin	09/01/1918	31/01/1918
Heading	War Diary of 2/3 West Riding Field Ambulance Volume XIV From Feb 1st 1918 To Feb 28th 1918		
War Diary	Anzin St Aubin	01/02/1918	10/02/1918
War Diary	Houvelin	11/02/1918	28/02/1918
Miscellaneous	Scheme Of Evacuation.	08/02/1918	08/02/1918
Map	Map		
Miscellaneous	Appendix 11 Progress of Work on Camp Site at Anzin.		
Diagram etc	Stone Wall		
Miscellaneous	Programme Of Training	26/02/1918	26/02/1918
Heading	War Diary Of 2/3 West Riding Field Ambulance March 1918 Volume XV		
War Diary	Houvelin	01/03/1918	02/03/1918
War Diary	Anzin	03/03/1918	23/03/1918
War Diary	Arras	24/03/1918	25/03/1918
War Diary	Bucquoy	26/03/1918	26/03/1918
War Diary	Humbercamp	27/03/1918	31/03/1918
Heading	War Diary Of 2/3 West Riding Field Ambulance Volume XV April 1918		
War Diary	Humbercamp	01/04/1918	01/04/1918
War Diary	Marieux	02/04/1918	07/04/1918
War Diary	Bienvillers	08/04/1918	24/04/1918
War Diary	Authie	25/04/1918	30/04/1918
Miscellaneous	Appendix I Evacuation of Wounded from the IVth Corps Left Divisional Front.	10/04/1918	10/04/1918
Miscellaneous	Appendix 2.	24/04/1918	24/04/1918
Heading	War Diary Of 2/3rd West Riding Field Ambulance May 1918 Volume XVII		
War Diary	Authie	01/05/1918	17/05/1918
War Diary	Pas	18/05/1918	31/05/1918
Diagram etc	To Authie		

Heading	War Diary Of 2/3rd West Riding Field Ambulance June 1918 Volume XVIII		
War Diary	Pas	01/06/1918	25/06/1918
War Diary	Terrasmesnil	26/06/1918	30/06/1918
Miscellaneous	Appendix 1 Admissions for P.U.O. and influenza.		
Heading	War Diary Of 2/3 West Riding Field Ambulance July 1918 Volume XIX		
War Diary	Terramesnil	01/07/1918	15/07/1918
War Diary	Mailly Le Grand	16/07/1918	16/07/1918
War Diary	Ecury Sur Coole	17/07/1918	18/07/1918
War Diary	Vertus	19/07/1918	19/07/1918
War Diary	Sezanne	20/07/1918	20/07/1918
War Diary	Champillon	21/07/1918	24/07/1918
War Diary	Serimer	25/07/1918	27/07/1918
War Diary	Pourcy	28/07/1918	30/07/1918
War Diary	St Moges	31/07/1918	31/07/1918
Miscellaneous	Programme Of Training		
Miscellaneous	Evacuation From 185th Infantry Brigade		
Miscellaneous	Appendix 3 Arrangement for evacuation from the LEFT SECTOR in Conjunction With the 51st Division.		
Miscellaneous	Appendix 4		
Miscellaneous	Appendix 4 Line of Evacuation 28th July, 1918.	28/07/1918	28/07/1918
Heading	War Diary Of 2/3 West Riding Field Amb August 1918 Vol XX		
War Diary	St Imoges	01/08/1918	01/08/1918
War Diary	Cite Auban Mouet	02/08/1918	05/08/1918
War Diary	Mont Renault Fm	06/08/1918	20/08/1918
War Diary	Saulty	21/08/1918	22/08/1918
War Diary	Mont Renault Farm	23/08/1918	23/08/1918
War Diary	Doullens	24/08/1918	24/08/1918
War Diary	Bienvillers	25/08/1918	28/08/1918
War Diary	Ayette	29/08/1918	31/08/1918
Heading	War Diary Of 2/3rd West Riding Field Ambulance September 1918 Volume XXI		
War Diary	Ayette	01/09/1918	01/09/1918
War Diary	Courcelles	02/09/1918	09/09/1918
War Diary	Behagnies	10/09/1918	11/09/1918
War Diary	Royalcourt	12/09/1918	16/09/1918
War Diary	Behagnies	17/09/1918	25/09/1918
War Diary	Bertincourt	26/09/1918	28/09/1918
War Diary	Yorkshire Bank	29/09/1918	30/09/1918
Miscellaneous	Appendix I And Appendix II		
Miscellaneous	Appendix I Line of Evacuation First Phase.		
Miscellaneous	Appendix 2 Line of Evacuation First Phase.		
Map	Part Of Sheets 57C n e 57 C1/20000		
Miscellaneous	Appendix III		
Miscellaneous	Appendix III Operations 27th September, 1918 to 30th September, 1918.	27/09/1918	27/09/1918
Map	Map		
Heading	War Diary Of 2/3 West Riding Field Ambulance October 1918 Volume XXII		
War Diary	Ribecourt	01/10/1918	01/10/1918
War Diary	Yorkshire Bank	02/10/1918	09/10/1918
War Diary	Ribecourt	10/10/1918	10/10/1918
War Diary	Rumilly	11/10/1918	11/10/1918
War Diary	Boistrancourt	12/10/1918	13/10/1918

War Diary	Cattenieres	14/10/1918	19/10/1918
War Diary	Bevillers	20/10/1918	23/10/1918
War Diary	Carnieres	24/10/1918	31/10/1918
Heading	War Diary of 2/3 West Riding Field Ambulance From November 1st 1918 To November 30th 1918 Volume XXIII		
War Diary	Carnieres	01/11/1918	02/11/1918
War Diary	Solesmes	03/11/1918	05/11/1918
War Diary	Ruesnes	06/11/1918	07/11/1918
War Diary	Orsinval	08/11/1918	08/11/1918
War Diary	Gommegnies	09/11/1918	10/11/1918
War Diary	Quene Loup	11/11/1918	12/11/1918
War Diary	Sous Le Bois	13/11/1918	18/11/1918
War Diary	Ostergnies	19/11/1918	19/11/1918
War Diary	Montignies	20/11/1918	20/11/1918
War Diary	Gozee	21/11/1918	24/11/1918
War Diary	Joncret	25/11/1918	25/11/1918
War Diary	Mettet	26/11/1918	26/11/1918
War Diary	Warnant	27/11/1918	27/11/1918
War Diary	Sorinnes	28/11/1918	30/11/1918
Heading	War Diary of 2/3rd West Riding Field Ambulance From 1.12.1918 To 31.12.1918 Volume XXIV		
War Diary	Sorinnes	01/12/1918	09/12/1918
War Diary	Auwez	10/12/1918	11/12/1918
War Diary	Mean	12/12/1918	12/12/1918
War Diary	Himbe	13/12/1918	13/12/1918
War Diary	My	14/12/1918	14/12/1918
War Diary	Haute Bodeux	15/12/1918	16/12/1918
War Diary	Stavelot	17/12/1918	17/12/1918
War Diary	Weywertz	17/12/1918	20/12/1918
War Diary	Mont Joie	21/12/1918	22/12/1918
War Diary	Schowe-Seiffen	22/12/1918	22/12/1918
War Diary	Hergarten	23/12/1918	31/12/1918
Heading	War Diary of 2/3rd West Riding Field Ambulance From January 1st 1919 To January 31st 1919 Volume XXV		
War Diary	Hergarten	01/01/1919	31/01/1919
Heading	War Diary of 2/3rd West Riding Field Ambulance From 1st February 1919 To 28th February 1919 Volume XXVI		
War Diary	Hergarten	01/02/1919	19/02/1919
War Diary	Germany	20/02/1919	28/02/1919
Heading	War Diary of 2/3rd West Riding Field Ambulance From 1st March 1919 To 31st March 1919 Volume XXVII		
War Diary	Hergarten	01/03/1919	01/03/1919
War Diary	Germany	02/03/1919	06/03/1919
War Diary	Girbelsrath	07/03/1919	07/03/1919
War Diary	Germany	08/03/1919	17/03/1919
War Diary	Girbelsrath	18/03/1919	18/03/1919
War Diary	Germany	18/03/1919	31/03/1919
Heading	War Diary of 2/3rd West Riding Field Ambulance From 1st April 1919 To 30th April 1919 Volume XXVIII		
War Diary	Girbelsrath	01/04/1919	30/04/1919
Heading	War Diary of 2/3 West Riding Field Amb From May 1st 1919 To May 31st 1919 Volume XXIX		
War Diary	Girblesrath	01/05/1919	22/05/1919
War Diary	Duren	23/05/1919	31/05/1919

Heading	War Diary of 2/3rd West Riding Field Ambulance From 1/6/1919 To 30/6/1919 Volume XXX		
War Diary	Duren	01/06/1919	16/06/1919
War Diary	Ohligs	17/06/1919	30/06/1919
Heading	War Diary of 2/3rd West Riding Field Ambulance From 1-7-1919 To 31-7-1919 Volume XXXI		
War Diary	Ohligs	01/07/1919	01/07/1919
War Diary	Duren	02/07/1919	30/07/1919
Heading	2/3rd West Riding Field Ambulance		
War Diary	Duren	01/08/1919	15/08/1919
War Diary	Calais	16/08/1919	16/08/1919
War Diary	London	17/08/1919	17/08/1919
War Diary	Gattenich Camp	18/08/1919	22/08/1919
War Diary	Clipstone Camp	23/08/1919	31/08/1919

W095/30783/3

62ND DIVISION

2-3RD (W.R.) FLD AMBULANCE
JAN 1917-DEC 1918
1919, AUG

Army Form C. 2118

WAR DIARY
or
INTELLIGENCE SUMMARY

(Erase heading not required.)

140/944.

Vol 1

Confidential

War Diary

of

2/3rd West Riding Field Ambulance

from 10th Jany 1917 to 31st Jany 1917.

(Volume 1.)

COMMITTEE FOR THE
MEDICAL HISTORY OF THE WAR
Date 13 MAR. 1917

ORIGINAL

Army Form C. 2118.

WAR DIARY
or
INTELLIGENCE SUMMARY

23rd N.R. Field Ambulance No. 1.

(Erase heading not required.)

Instructions regarding War Diaries and Intelligence Summaries are contained in F.S. Regs., Part II. and the Staff Manual respectively. Title pages will be prepared in manuscript.

Place	Date	Hour	Summary of Events and Information	Remarks and references to Appendices
Wellingborough	10/1/17	3 A.M	Unit entrained at Wellingborough en route for Southampton.	
La Havre	12/1/17	5 A.M	Unit arrived and "camped" the night at No. 2 Rest Camp.	J.F. Barrett
	13/1/17	Noon	Unit entrained for Frévent.	
RANSART	14/1/17	4 p.m	Unit arrived. Officers and men billetted. Horses picketed in the open. A.D.M.S.M.I. 14-1-17	
RANSART	15/1/17		Retention Hospital opened. (Authority A.D.M.S.M.I. 14-1-17)	
RANSART	16-1-17		Seven motor ambulances (5 Daimlers and 2 "Fords") and one motor cycle with personnel arrive and report for duty. Capt. Anthrone placed in charge.	J.F. Barrett
RANSART	17/1/17		The jerkins and second blankets issued to N.C.O.s and men. This was highly essential, owing to the extreme cold and the men coming straight from billets in private houses to the huts as now provided. (ruined buildings etc.)	J.F. Barrett
			System of baths for the unit instituted.	
RANSART	19/1/17		A composite Section reported to the A.D.M.S. 32nd Division for instruction, and were attached to the 91st & 92nd Field Ambulances	J.F. Barrett
RANSART	20/1/17			

Army Form C. 2118.

WAR DIARY

No. 2

or
INTELLIGENCE SUMMARY.
3rd W Field Ambulance.

(Erase heading not required.)

Instructions regarding War Diaries and Intelligence Summaries are contained in F.S. Regs., Part II. and the Staff Manual respectively. Title pages will be prepared in manuscript.

Place	Date	Hour	Summary of Events and Information	Remarks and references to Appendices
			Continued	
RANSART	22/1/17		Officers attending were Capt. E. White, Capt. J.M. Pringle and Lt Wm Fy Burton.	
			Unit derived joins the 187th Inf Bde. marched to BEAUVAL and "hick" the night there.	
BEAUVAL	23/1/17	9.30AM	Unit leaves, marches to LOUVENCOURT, to new station recently vacated by the 92nd Field Ambulance.	
LOUVENCOURT	23/1/17		Detention Hospital opened	
-do-	24/1/17		Lieut & Qm. B.H. Burton recalled to Unit for duty from the 32nd Division.	
-do-	29/1/17		Composite Section return from the 32nd Division, and a second composite Section reports to the A.D.M.S. 32nd Division	
-do-	29/1/17		for instruction. Officers attending, Captains W.W.J. Lenane + W Luclair MR. Kaurely	
-do-	30/1/17		Lieut Col. W.P. Kell admitted to officers Hospital at AUTHIE, as a patient.	
-do-	31/1/17		Major H.M. Barnett reports to the A.D.M.S 32nd Division for a course of instruction.	

ORIGINAL

Feb. 1917 40/994

62nd Div Vol 2

— CONFIDENTIAL —

— DIARY —

OF

2/3rd W. R. FIELD AMBULANCE.

From:- 1st Feb. 1917. To:- 28th Feb. 1917.

Volume II

[COMMITTEE FOR THE
HISTORICAL HISTORY OF THE WAR
Date 4 – APR.1917]

WAR DIARY — 2/3rd W.R. Field Ambulance

Army Form C. 2118.

Volume II — (Sheet I)
February 1917.

INTELLIGENCE SUMMARY.
(Erase heading not required.)

Place	Date	Hour	Summary of Events and Information	Remarks and references to Appendices
LOUVENCOURT	3/2/17		MAJOR N. BARNETT, returned from a course of instruction with the 32nd Division.	App 3
—do.—	4/2/17		A third composite Section of this unit, reported to the A.D.M.S. 32nd Division for a course of instruction. Officers attending:— Capt. F. WIGGLESWORTH, Capt. R.P. ANDERSON, and Lieut. W. STAPPARD.	App 3
—do.—	4/2/17		The second composite Section returned from a course of instruction with the Field Ambulances of the 32nd Division.	App B
—do.—	6/2/17		Officers Rest Hospital of I. Corps taken over by this Unit.	App 5
—do.—	11/2/17		The third composite Section returned from a course of instruction with the Field Ambulances of the 32nd Division.	App B
Bus-le-Artois	16/2/17		Unit takes up new station. Capt. E. WHITE and 21. other ranks remain behind to work the I. Corps Officers Rest Hospital (LOUVENCOURT). Whilst the Unit was stationed at LOUVENCOURT, billets for N.C.O.s and men were improved. Additional bunking was erected. Repairs to the ten hospital huts were executed, and a slow combustion heating stove fitted in each.	App 10

Volume II (Sheet II) — WAR DIARY — 2/3rd W.R. Field Ambulance Army Form C. 2118.
February 1917 — INTELLIGENCE SUMMARY.

ORIGINAL.

Place	Date	Hour	Summary of Events and Information	Remarks and references to Appendices
FORCEVILLE	23/2/17		The Unit takes up new station here.	
—do.—			A hospital for the sick of the 62nd Division, and those sick of other Divisions of the V Corps, who come to it from the Lines, is opened.	WWB

Maurice Burnett
O/C. 2/3rd W.R. Field Ambulance
RAMC

62nd. Division

Mar. 1917 140/2042
CONFIDENTIAL. — Vol 3

WAR DIARY OF

2/3rd. W. R. FIELD AMBULANCE.

From :- 1st March 1917
To :- 31st March 1917.

COMMITTEE FOR THE
MEDICAL HISTORY OF THE WAR
Date 11 MAY. 1917

VOLUME. 3.

App I detached &
put with summary.

Original.

WAR DIARY
2/3rd N.R. Field Ambulance.
INTELLIGENCE SUMMARY. — March, 1917 — Sheet I.

Army Form C. 2118.

(Erase heading not required.)

Place	Date	Hour	Summary of Events and Information	Remarks and references to Appendices
Forceville	1/3/17		Beds for patients were improvised by placing stretchers on wood trestles. The trestles as per the attached sketch were made regimentally.	Sketch NO.KM/91 1639.
—do—	6/3/17		The hospital from this date is a Scabies Hospital for the V. Corps.	do
—do—	6/3/17		Driver T.4/253790. Burnell M. evacuated to C.C.S.	do
—do—	8/3/17		Capt. N. SNEDDON, discharged from the V. Corps Officers Rest Hospital, and re reported to this Unit for duty the same day.	do
—do—	14/3/17		Capt. F WIGGLESWORTH and a bearer sub-division from this unit report for duty to the 2/1st W.R. Field Ambulance. Pte 136. SINGLETON, T. of this party did excellent work, and a report from the M.O./C. mentions an instance where this man airplayed unusual coolness and courage under shell fire. A copy of the report referred to is attached.	K.M./98 1684
—do—	14/3/17		Capt. J.M. PRINGLE detached from this unit temporarily, to do duty as M.O. to the 2/5 & 2/3 West Yorkshire Regt.	do
—do—	16/3/17		Pte. W.H. STOCKS No.1886. evacuated to C.C.S.	do

WAR DIARY
or
INTELLIGENCE SUMMARY.

2/3rd W.R. Field Ambulance. Army Form C. 2118.
— March. 1917. —
— Sheet. II. —

Place	Date	Hour	Summary of Events and Information	Remarks and references to Appendices
Forceville.	23/3/17.		Pte. 1852 PEARSON, J.W. evacuated to O.C.C.S.	
—do.—	25/3/17.		Capt. N. SHARRARD. attached temporarily for duty with the 2/2nd W.R. Field Ambulance.	
—do.—	26/3/17.		Capt. F. WIGGESWORTH and bearer sub-division rejoin the unit from the 3/1st W.R. Field Ambulance.	
—do.—	27/3/17.		The V Corps Officers Rest Hospital at LOUVENCOURT closed. Capt. E. WHITE and personnel rejoin the unit.	
—do.—	29-3-17.		Major W. CROLY, R.A.M.C. reported for duty as Commanding Officer of the Unit.	

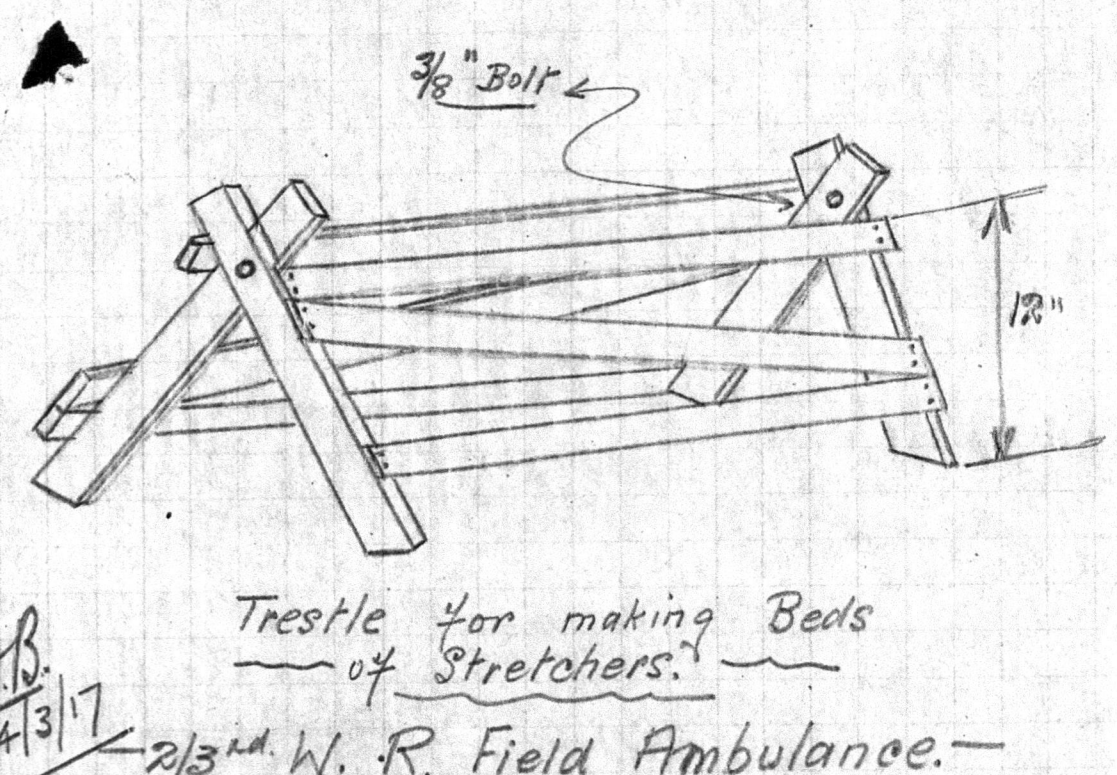

Trestle for making Beds of Stretchers.

2/3rd W. R. Field Ambulance.

O.B. 4/3/17

Oct. 1917

S

62nd Divn.

2/3rd West Riding F.A.

140/2086

COMMITTEE FOR THE
MEDICAL HISTORY OF THE WAR
Date -6 JUN.1917

ORIGINAL

CONFIDENTIAL. Vol 4

WAR DIARY OF

2/3rd. W.R. Field Ambulance.

From:- 1st April 1917.   To:- 30th April 1917.

VOLUME. IV.

ORIGINAL.

WAR DIARY — 2/3rd W.R. Field Ambulance. Army Form C. 2118.
or
INTELLIGENCE SUMMARY. — Sheet. I — April. 1917.—

(Erase heading not required.)

Instructions regarding War Diaries and Intelligence Summaries are contained in F.S. Regs., Part II. and the Staff Manual respectively. Title pages will be prepared in manuscript.

Place	Date	Hour	Summary of Events and Information	Remarks and references to Appendices
FORCEVILLE.	3/4/17		I. Corps Rest Hospital at Achieux taken over from the 2/2nd. W.R. Field Ambulance.	
—do.—	3/4/17		A bearer sub-division of this unit report to the 2/3rd W.R Field Ambulance for duty	
—do.—	5/4/17		Capt. W. SHARRARD (who was temporarily attached for duty with the 2/2nd. W.R. Field Ambulance) is, from this date transferred, temporarily, to the 2/4 D.B. Y & L Regt. no medical officer to the battalion.	
—do.—	9/4/17.		Lieut. H. J. SIMSON, R.A.M.C. reported for duty with the unit. He is attached to the unit as a reinforcement.	
—do.—	9/4/17		I. Corps Rest Hospital at Achieux, handed over to the 2/3rd. Home Counties Field Ambulance.	
—do.—	10/4/17.		An advance party of 60 men in charge of Capt. F. WIGGLESWORTH and Capt. R.P. ANDERSON proceed to BIHUCOURT to take over from the 2/3rd W.R. Field Ambulance.	
—do.—	11/4/17.		A bearer sub-division is held in reserve at BIHUCOURT, in compliance with 62nd Div. R.A.M.C. operation order No. 13. Extract copy attached.	R.M/9./1695.

WAR DIARY - 2/3rd N.R. Field Ambulance - Army Form C. 2118.

April 1917 — Sheet II.

Instructions regarding War Diaries and Intelligence Summaries are contained in F.S. Regs., Part II. and the Staff Manual respectively. Title pages will be prepared in manuscript.

INTELLIGENCE SUMMARY.
(Erase heading not required.)

Place	Date	Hour	Summary of Events and Information	Remarks and references to Appendices
FORCEVILLE	11/4/17		V. Corps Scabies Hospital closed.	
-do.-	12/4/17	9.A.M.	Unit proceeds by road to BIHUCOURT to new station, all ranks & motor cars.	
-do.-	12/4/17		Stores etc. at the Scabies Hospital, handed over to the 2/3rd Home Counties Field Ambulance.	
BIHUCOURT	14/4/17	12.noon	Camp moved to a site near to ACHIET-LE-GRAND, owing to this camp being shelled by the German artillery.	
ACHIET-LE-GRAND.	14/4/17		A Divisional Detention Hospital for sick opened.	
-do.-	20/4/17		Lieut. H.J. SIMSON (R.A.M.C.) is attached from the unit for duty as M.O. to the Divisional Retail.	
-do.-	22/4/17		Capt. G.W. BERESFORD (R.A.M.C.) reported to the unit for duty.	
-do.-	25/4/17		Capt. G.W. BERESFORD (R.A.M.C.) detached for duty as M.O. to the 310th Brigade R.F.A.	
-do.-	25/4/17		Capt. J.A. HARTLEY (R.A.M.C.) reported to the unit for duty.	
-do.-	30/4/17		Capt. R.P. ANDERSON (R.A.M.C.) transferred sick to Officers Hospital, Wimereux.	

Secret.

K.M./Q/.1645.
2/3rd W.R. Field Amb"

Extract from

Operation Order R.A.M.C. 62nd Division No. 13.

Copy No. 18.

9th April, 1917.

Para. 3. Extract.

Two Bearer sub-divisions will be held in Reserve at H...a,6.4. (One each by the 2/1st and 2/3rd West Riding Field Ambulances).

- Signed - de B. Birch,
Colonel, A.M.S. (T.)
C.O. R.A.M.C., 62nd Division.

May 1917

62nd Div.

2/3rd West Riding F.A.

COMMITTEE FOR THE
MEDICAL HISTORY OF THE WAR
Date 10 JUL. 1917

— ORIGINAL —

— CONFIDENTIAL —

Vol 5

WAR DIARY OF
2/3rd West Riding Field Ambulance

From 1st May 1917 To:- 31st May 1917

VOLUME V.

WAR DIARY – 2/3rd W. R. Field ambulance

INTELLIGENCE SUMMARY. – May 1917. – Sheet I –

Army Form C. 2118.

(Erase heading not required.)

Place	Date	Hour	Summary of Events and Information	Remarks and references to Appendices
ACHIET-LE-GRAND	1-5-17	–	A bearer sub-division of this unit reported to the 92nd W.R. Field Ambulance for duty.	
–do –	6/5/17	–	Lieut. R.O. HUTCHINSON (R.A.M.C) reported to the unit for duty.	2A
–do –	7/5/17	–	Capt. J.H. HARTLEY (R.A.M.C.) leaves the unit and reports to the A.D.M.S. ABBEVILLE for duty.	2A
–do –	7/5/17	–	Lieut R.O. HUTCHINSON (R.A.M.C) detached and reported for duty to the 312th Brigade. R.F.A.	2A
–do.	11/5/17	–	Capt. R.P. ANDERSON (R.A.M.C) reported his arrival for duty, from the Officers Hospital, Warloy.	2A
–do.–	12/5/17	–	The hospital complete (less mobilization equipment) is handed over to the 23rd Field Ambulance.	2A
Buequoy.	13/5/17	–	Unit arrived and took over Detention Hospital from the 23rd Field Ambulance.	2A
–do.–	14/5/17	–	Capt. R.P. ANDERSON, R.A.M.C. is detached for temporary duty as M.O. to the No. 1. Heavy Artillery Brigade Group.	2A
–do.–	15/5/17	–	The two bearer sub-divisions of this unit, that were temporarily	2A

WAR DIARY — 3/2nd W.R. Field Ambulance — Sheet II

Army Form C. 2118.

INTELLIGENCE SUMMARY. May 1917.

Place	Date	Hour	Summary of Events and Information	Remarks and references to Appendices
BUCQUOY.			— continued —	
	15/5/17		attached to the 3/2nd W.R. Field Ambulance for duty, are from this date transferred to the M.D.S. MORY, under the administration of the 58th Division.	
BUCQUOY.	15/5/17.		Capt. W.W.J. LAWSON (R.A.M.C) and 45 other ranks, attached for temporary duty at the M.D.S. MORY (58th Division).	
BUCQUOY.	15/5/17		Major H.N. BARNETT (R.A.M.C) and 21 other ranks detached for temporary duty at the 7 Corps Rest Station, ACHIET-LE-GRAND.	
BUCQUOY.	16/5/17		Unit hands over hospital complete to the 21st Field Ambulance and moves to new site at COURCELLES.	
COURCELLES.	18/5/17.		No. 45. C.C.S. report that Pte. 91. FAIREST A. of this Unit, died of wounds on the 17th inst. (This man was temporarily attached for duty to the M.D.S. MORY).	
— do. —	18/5/17		O/C. Main Dressing Station, MORY, reports that the undermentioned men of this Unit were interred on the 17th inst. Pte. 73. HUMBERSTONE W., Pte. 91. FAIREST A. (See previous entry.) Pte. 1809. COLLINS A.L. and Pte. 1815. GUNNER G.B.	
— do. —	19/5/17.		Capt. R.R. ANDERSON (R.A.M.C) returned to the Unit from W.I. Heavy Artillery Group.	

WAR DIARY — 2/3rd W.R. Field Ambulance. — Army Form C. 2118.
INTELLIGENCE SUMMARY — May 1917 — Sheet III

Place	Date	Hour	Summary of Events and Information	Remarks and references to Appendices
COURCELLES.	19/5/17		A.D.M.S. reports that Capt. W.M.J. LAWSON (R.A.M.C.) of this Unit became a Batt. casualty "shell concussion" whilst doing duty at M.D.S. He has been evacuated to No. 49. C.C.S.	LA
-do-	20/5/17		O/c. M.D.S. MORY. reports that Pte. 1929. CORDON. H. is suffering from shell shock, and that he was admitted to No. 47. C.C.S. on the 19th inst.	LA
-do-	18/5/17		O/c. M.D.S. MORY. reports that Sergt. 1833. MAY. J. was evacuated to C.C.S. ACHIET-LE-GRAND. 18-5-17 having been gassed.	LA
-do-	18/5/17		O/c. M.D.S. MORY. reports that Sergt. 397. PARDOE. C. has been wounded, and evacuated to C.C.S. ACHIET-LE-GRAND. on the 18-5-17. J.W.	LA
-do-	23/5/17		O/c. M.D.S. MORY. reports that Sergt. 365. GALLIMORE. A was killed in action on the 22nd inst. this Unit arranged for the burial at MORY. J.W.	LA
-do-	23/5/17		O/c. M.D.S. MORY. reports that Pte. 90. ELLIS. it was wounded on the 22nd inst. and transferred to C.C.S. ACHIET-LE-GRAND. same day.	LA
-do-	23/5/17		Capt. P.H. RAWSON. M.C. (R.A.M.C.) reported his arrival jointly with this Unit.	LA
-do-	24/5/17		TWELVE REINFORCEMENTS. JOINED THE UNIT FROM CYCLISTS' BASE DEPOT.	LA

Army Form C. 2118.

WAR DIARY or INTELLIGENCE SUMMARY.

2/3rd W.R. Field Ambulance — MAY 1917 — SHEET IV

(Erase heading not required.)

Instructions regarding War Diaries and Intelligence Summaries are contained in F.S. Regs., Part II. and the Staff Manual respectively. Title pages will be prepared in manuscript.

Place	Date	Hour	Summary of Events and Information	Remarks and references to Appendices
COURCELLES	25/5/17			
-do-	24/5/17		Twelve additional bearers sent to M.D.S. MORY. Captain R.P. ANDERSON, RAMC(T) is detached for temporary duty as M.O. i/c 2/8. West Yorkshire Regiment.	
-do-	25/5/17		Officer i/c M.D.S. MORY reports that the undermentioned men have been wounded and evacuated to C.C.S. Achiet-le-Grand. No 405297 Pte PALFREYMAN, W.E. and No 138 Pte BURKINSHAW, G. Unit lorries Courcelles and proceeds to GOMIECOURT.	
-do-	29/5/17		64 Other ranks return from the lines for duty with the Field Ambulance	
GOMIECOURT	29/5/17			
-do-	30/5/17		Notification received from O.C. 45 C.C.S. Hut No 90 Private LEWIS, H. died of wounds 30th May 1917.	

W.G.M.
Lt.Colonel
2/3 W.R. Field Ambulance

1/6/17

14
June 1917

ORIGINAL

CONFIDENTIAL 140/230

WAR DIARY

of 2/3 WEST RIDING FIELD AMBULANCE

VOLUME VI — JUNE 1917

COMMITTEE FOR THE
MEDICAL HISTORY OF THE WAR
Date — 7 AUG. 1917

In the Field

WAR DIARY
2/3rd N.R. FIELD Ambulance — JUNE 1917 — Sheet 1

INTELLIGENCE SUMMARY

Place	Date	Hour	Summary of Events and Information	Remarks and references to Appendices
GOMIECOURT	1/6/17		The Military Medal awarded to No. 405444. Pte. E. THORNTON by the I. Corps Commander, for working continuously throughout the fight 20th-21st May 1917. at BULLECOURT, unceasingly wounded from the Regimental Aid Post, which was continuously shelled heavy shell fire and full of cases awaiting evacuation, by his courageous example and devotion to duty, all cases awaiting evacuation were successfully cleared before morning. Three times he went through a heavy barrage to obtain additional stretcher bearers.	
GOMIECOURT	3/6/17		The Military Medal awarded to No. 405309. Pte. GEORGE. S. HARRIS. for displaying the greatest resourcefulness and devotion to duty in returning to the wounded and getting the rest of the men under cover when the Advanced Dressing Station known as O'REILLYS POST, near BULLECOURT, was blown in by shell fire, killing and wounding all occupants on the 22-5-17. It was mainly due to the skilful manner in which this man acted that the casualties were not heavier, the shell fire at the time being very heavy.	

Army Form C. 2118.

WAR DIARY — 2/3rd N.R. Field Ambulance. —
or
INTELLIGENCE SUMMARY. — June. 1917. — Sheet II —
(Erase heading not required.)

Instructions regarding War Diaries and Intelligence Summaries are contained in F.S. Regs., Part II. and the Staff Manual respectively. Title pages will be prepared in manuscript.

Place	Date	Hour	Summary of Events and Information	Remarks and references to Appendices
GOMIECOURT	4/6/17.		Capt. R.P. ANDERSON returned from detached duty with the 2/2D WEST YORKSHIRE REGT.	LA
-do-	5/6/17.		A reinforcement party of ten (10) men from Cyclist Base Depot, reported their arrival.	LA
-do-	7/6/17.		A tent sub-division from this unit sent to the V Corps Rest Station, ACHIET-LE-GRAND, for duty.	LA
-do-	8/6/17.		Capt. P.H. RANSON, detailed for temporary duty with the 2/2nd W.R. Field Ambulance in compliance with A.D.M.S. instructions.	LA
-do-	9/6/17.		The tent sub-division detached for temporary duty on the 12 May/17 rejoined the unit to-day.	LA
-do-	10/6/17.		Capt. R.P. ANDERSON, detailed for temporary duty as M.O. to the 2/5-th Batt, Y & L Regt.	LA
-do-	10/6/17.		Ten (other ranks) men of this unit proceed to V. Army Summer Rest Camp at VALERY-SUR-SOMME, for rest.	LA
-do-	14/6/17.		Captain H.N. BARNETT (R.A.M.C.T.) is taken off the strength of this unit from this date in accordance with G.R.O. 2348 (para. e) Authority :— 62nd DIV. A/6772/8. (14-6-17.)	LA

T2134. Wt. W708—776. 500000. 4/15. Sir J. C. & S.

Army Form C. 2118.

WAR DIARY
or
INTELLIGENCE SUMMARY.

2/3rd West Riding Field Ambulance
Title — 111
June 1917 — Sheet 1

Instructions regarding War Diaries and Intelligence Summaries are contained in F. S. Regs., Part II. and the Staff Manual respectively. Title pages will be prepared in manuscript.

(Erase heading not required.)

Place	Date	Hour	Summary of Events and Information	Remarks and references to Appendices
GOMIECOURT	21/6/17		Lieutenant-Colonel W. CROLY (Officer Commanding this Unit) leaves the unit to report to D.D.M.S. BOULOGNE for duty. Captain E. Wilde R.A.M.C. takes temporary Command of Unit.	Eiv.
-do-	21/6/17		No 405359 Corporal WRIGHT. A. proceeds to Brigade as Sanitary Officer Corps Unit	Eiv
-do-	22/6/17		Captain R.P. ANDERSON. R.A.M.C.T. returned to unit from 2/5. Y + L	Eiv
-do-	24/6/17		Lieutenant H.T SIMPSON. R.A.M.C (T.C.) is taken off the strength of the unit from this date. Authority V.A./13+/463. V Corps dated 17-6-17: D.D.M.S. V Corps P.147/788/17 dated 22-6-17.	Eiv
FAVREUIL	27/6/17		Unit leaves GOMIECOURT and proceeds to FAVREUIL and takes over Hospital Site at H.16.d.9.6, the Dressing Station at C.20.d.25, wagon Post C.15.a.98. Collecting Station at C.10.c.7.8, Relay Post C.11.a.4.6, Regimental Aid Posts at C.5.a.3.2 and C.5.d.7.8. from the 60th Field Ambulance 20th Division. Sketch of the new area is attached. The unit is responsible for the evacuation of wounded	Eiv

T2134. Wt. W708—776. 500000. 4/15. Sir J. C. & S.

Army Form C. 2118.

WAR DIARY
or
INTELLIGENCE SUMMARY.

2/3rd West-Riding Field Ambulance

June 1917 — Sheet IV

(Erase heading not required.)

Instructions regarding War Diaries and Intelligence Summaries are contained in F. S. Regs., Part II. and the Staff Manual respectively. Title pages will be prepared in manuscript.

Place	Date	Hour	Summary of Events and Information	Remarks and references to Appendices
FAVREUIL	27/6/17		from the left sector of the line from 5 P.M. this date.	Civ
do			Captain P. H. RAWSON. M.C. Rejoins the unit from 2/5. K.O.Y.L.I.	
do	29/6/17		Captain T. C. YOUNG. R.A.M.C. (S.R) reports to the unit for duty from 13. General Hospital	Civ
-do-	29/6/17		Hon. Lieutenant and Quartermaster O. F. BUXTON leaves the unit, proceeds to England to join Ordnance College	Civ
				Civil emci

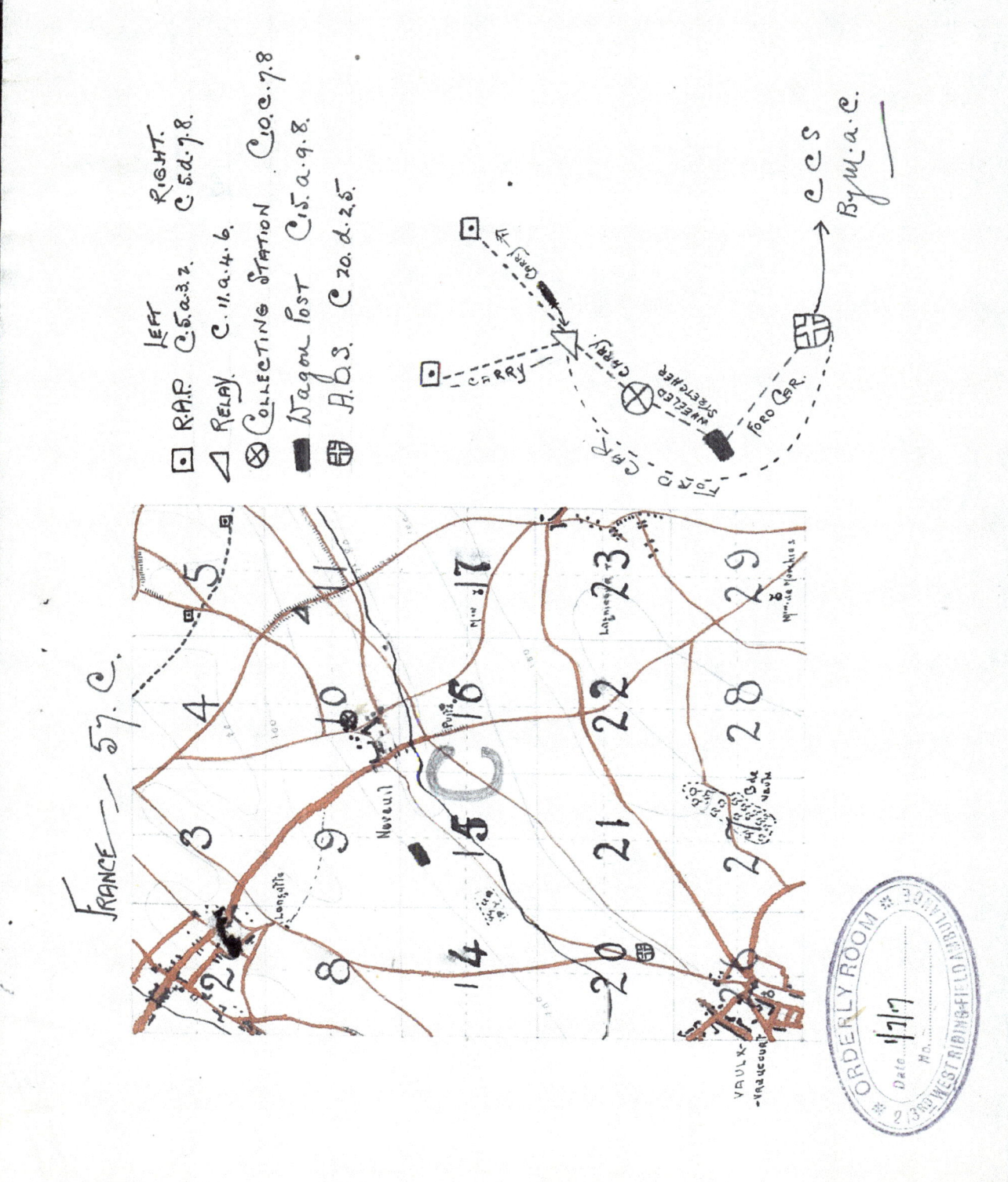

CONFIDENTIAL

WAR DIARY

2/3 West Riding Field Ambulance

July. 1917.

VOLUME 7

ORIGINAL

COMMITTEE FOR THE
MEDICAL HISTORY OF THE WAR
Date 10 SEP.1917

Army Form C. 2118.

WAR DIARY
or
INTELLIGENCE SUMMARY.

2/3 West Riding Field Ambulance

July 1917 SHEET 1

Place	Date	Hour	Summary of Events and Information	Remarks and references to Appendices
FAVREUIL	4/7/17		Major P. G. WILLIAMSON. M.C. R.A.M.C. reported his arrival and assumed command of the Field Ambulance from this date	BfW
-do-			Captain E. WHITE. R.A.M.C. leaves the unit to report to I Corps Headquarters. He is taken off the strength of the unit from this date.	BfW
-do-	5/7/17		D.D.M.S. V Corps visited the Camp.	BfW
-do-	6/7/17		Nothing to report.	BfW
			I visited the forward area and inspected the R.A.P.'s + Relay collecting posts	BfW
-do-	7/7/17		The Acting D.D.M.S. VI Corps visited the Camp.	BfW
-do-	8/7/17		Nothing to report.	BfW
-do-	9/7/17		Nothing to report.	BfW
-do-	10/7/17		Visited the A.D.S.	BfW
-do-	11/7/17		Acting A.D.M.S. 62nd Division visited the Camp.	BfW
-do-	12/7/17		Nothing to report.	BfW

T2134. Wt. W708—776. 500000. 4/15. Sir J. C. & S.

Army Form C. 2118.

WAR DIARY
or
INTELLIGENCE SUMMARY.
(Erase heading not required.)

2/3 West Riding Field Ambulance

SHEET 1

Instructions regarding War Diaries and Intelligence Summaries are contained in F.S. Regs., Part II. and the Staff Manual respectively. Title pages will be prepared in manuscript.

Place	Date	Hour	Summary of Events and Information	Remarks and references to Appendices
FAVREUIL	13/7/17	—	Visited A.D.S. C.P. and left R.A.P.	Offw
- do -	14/7/17	—	Nothing to report	Offw
- do -	15/7/17		Nothing to Report	Offw
- do -	16/7/17		Nothing to Report	Offw
- do	17/7/17		A.D.M.S. 62nd Division visited the Camp	Offw
- do	18/7/17		Visited the A.D.S. G.O.C. 62nd Division visited the Camp.	Offw
- do -	19/7/17		A.D.M.S. Inspected the Camp. Nothing to report.	Offw
- do -	20/7/17		D.D.M.S. VI Corps with the A.D.M.S. 62nd Division visited the Camp.	Offw
- do -	21/7/17		Attended Conference at the office of D.D.M.S. VI Corps.	Offw
- do -	22/7/17		Nothing to report	Offw
- do -	23/7/17		Visited A.D.S. and Collecting Post	Offw
- do -	24/7/17		Nothing to report	Offw
- do -	25/7/17		Nothing to report	Offw
- do -	26/7/17		Visited the front area with the A.D.M.S.	Offw

Army Form C. 2118.

WAR DIARY
or
INTELLIGENCE SUMMARY.   2/3 West Riding Field Ambulance

SHEET III

(Erase heading not required.)

Instructions regarding War Diaries and Intelligence Summaries are contained in F.S. Regs., Part II. and the Staff Manual respectively. Title pages will be prepared in manuscript.

Place	Date	Hour	Summary of Events and Information	Remarks and references to Appendices
FAVREUIL	27/7/17		Nothing to Report	
do.	28/7/17		Nothing to Report.	
do.	29/7/17		Major P.G. Williamson, M.C. R.A.M.C. transferred (sick) to No. 3 C.C.S.	
- do -	30/7/17		Nothing to Report	
- do -	31/7/17		VI Corps Command inspected transport of the unit.	

J. Yeoman
Capt R.A.M.C.(T)

CONFIDENTIAL ORIGINAL

Aug. 1917.   140/2364.

WAR DIARY

Vol 8

of

2/3rd WEST RIDING FIELD AMBULANCE

VOLUME VIII — AUGUST. 1917

COMMITTEE FOR THE
MEDICAL HISTORY OF THE WAR
Date — 1 OCT. 1917

Army Form C. 2118.

WAR DIARY
or
INTELLIGENCE SUMMARY.
(Erase heading not required.)

2/3 West Riding Field Ambulance
August 1917. Sheet 1

Place	Date	Hour	Summary of Events and Information	Remarks and references to Appendices
FAVREUIL	1/8/17		ORIGINAL A.D.M.S. 62 Division Visited the Hospital.	JCY
-do-	2/8/17		Nothing to Report.	JCY
-do-	3/8/17		Nothing to Report.	JCY
-do-	4/8/17		Visited the forward area and inspected A.D.S. Wagon Post. Relieving Station, Relay Post and R.A.Ps. Quartermaster and Honorary Lieutenant H.M. BROWNE reported for duty with the Field Ambulance	JCY
-do-	5/8/17		Nothing to report	JCY
-do-	6/8/17		A.D.M.S. 62nd Division Visited the Camp.	JCY
-do-	7/8/17		Nothing to Report.	JCY
-do-	8/8/17		Instructions received from A.D.M.S. to strike Lieutenant H.J. SIMSON. R.A.M.C. T.C. off the strength of the Unit Authority D.D.M.S. VI Corps. M/2400/17 A.D.M.S. M/5518.	JCY
-do-	9/8/17		D.O.M.S. VI Corps visited the Hospital. Instructions received from the A.D.M.S. of the appointment of MAJOR. P.G. WILLIAMSON. M.C. to LIEUTENANT COLONEL while commanding	JCY

WAR DIARY or INTELLIGENCE SUMMARY

Army Form C. 2118.

2/3 West Riding Field Ambulance
August 1917. Sheet 1

Place	Date	Hour	Summary of Events and Information	Remarks and references to Appendices
FAVREUIL			(Continued).	
	9/8/17		2/3 West Riding Field Ambulance File for No. 146 of "Appointments Commissions, etc, approved by the Field Marshal Commanding-in-Chief".	JCW
-do-	10/8/17		Lieutenant T.R. Williams (United States Medical Corps) Reported for duty with the Field Ambulance	JCW
-do-	11/8/17		Nothing to Report	JCW
-do-	12/8/17		Lieutenant-Colonel P.G. Williamson, M.C. returned to the Unit from No 3. C.C.S.	JCW
			Lieutenant H. Hume. M.S.R.M.C. left the Unit to report to No 16. General Hospital	JCW
-do-	13/8/17		D.M.S. Third Army visited the Hospital and Camp. LE TREPORT	JCW
-do-	14/8/17		Nothing to Report	JCW
-do-	15/8/17		Nothing to Report	JCW
-do-	16/8/17		Visited the Advanced Dressing Station	JCW
-do-	17/8/17		A.D.M.S. 62nd Division visited the Camp	JCW
-do-	18/8/17		Corps Horse Show held	JCW

WAR DIARY or INTELLIGENCE SUMMARY

Army Form C. 2118.

2/3 West Riding Field Ambulance

SHEET 111

Place	Date	Hour	Summary of Events and Information	Remarks and references to Appendices
FAIRFUL	19/8/17		Advanced Dressing Station shelled with H.E. our R.A.M.C. Casualty (No 405) L/Cpl. THORPE, H.E.	
-do-	20/8/17		James Contrad THORPE Died at # 9 3 C.C.S.	GSW
-do-	21/8/17		Nothing to Report.	GSW
-do-	22/8/17		Nothing to Report.	GSW
-do-	23/8/17		A.D.M.S. 62 Division Visited the Camp.	GSW
-do-	24/8/17		Visited Advanced Dressing Station	GSW
-do-	25/8/17		Nothing to Report.	GSW
-do-	26/8/17		Nothing to Report.	GSW
-do-	27/8/17		Nothing to Report.	GSW
-do-	28/8/17		Lieutenant T.R. WILLIAMS. M.O.R.C. U.S.A. leaves the Unit to report to H.O.M.S. 7th Division. Captain T.M. BENSON. R.A.M.C. reported for duty with the Field Ambulance.	
-do-	29/8/17		A.D.M.S. 62nd Division Visited the Camp.	GSW
-do-	30/8/17		Lieutenant Colonel P. Williamson M.C. proceeded on leave to England	GSW

Army Form C. 2118.

WAR DIARY
or
INTELLIGENCE SUMMARY.   2/3 West Riding Field Ambulance   SHEET IV
(Erase heading not required.)

Place	Date	Hour	Summary of Events and Information	Remarks and references to Appendices
FAVREUIL	3/9/17		Nothing to Report J.b.Y	
			J.b.Young. Captain RAMC	
			For LIEUT COLONEL R.A.M.C.	
			COMMDG. 2/3rd. WEST RIDING FIELD AMBULANCE	

CONFIDENTIAL ORIGINAL

WAR DIARY Vol 9

of

2/3 WEST RIDING FIELD AMBULANCE

VOLUME IX

SEPTEMBER 1917

COMMITTEE FOR THE
MEDICAL HISTORY OF THE WAR
Date — 5 NOV. 1917

Army Form C. 2118.

WAR DIARY
or
INTELLIGENCE SUMMARY.

2/3 West Riding Field Ambulance

(Erase heading not required.)

SHEET 1

Instructions regarding War Diaries and Intelligence Summaries are contained in F.S. Regs, Part II. and the [?] Manual respectively. Title pages will be prepared in manuscript.

Place	Date	Hour	Summary of Events and Information	Remarks and references to Appendices
FAVREUIL	1/9/17		Nothing to Report	fcy
-Do-	2/9/17		ADMS visited the Camp. I visited A.D.S. and inspected all posts in the forward area	fcy
-Do-	3/9/17		Captain R.P. ANDERSON RAMC. rejoined the Unit from Hospital	fcy
-Do-	4/9/17		Nothing to Report	fcy
-Do-	5/9/17		Nothing to Report	fcy
-Do-	6/9/17		Captain F. WIGGLESWORTH detailed to attend Senior Officers Course at Divisional Gas School Sept. 7, 8, 10 and 11th 1917	fcy
-Do-	7/9/17		Nothing to Report	fcy
-Do-	8/9/17		Nothing to Report	fcy
-Do-	9/9/17		A.D.M.S. 62 Division visited the Camp. Captain P.H. RAWSON M.C. RAMC detailed to attend a two days Course at the Third Army Anti Gas School	fcy
-Do-	10/9/17		Lieutenant Colonel P.G. WILLIAMSON M.C. Returned from leave	fcy

Army Form C. 2118.

SHEET 1/1

WAR DIARY
or
INTELLIGENCE SUMMARY.
(Erase heading not required.)

2/3 West Riding Field Ambulance

Place	Date	Hour	Summary of Events and Information	Remarks and references to Appendices
FAVREUIL	11/9/17		Nothing to Report.	
-do-	13/9/17		Tested P.O.S. and Collecting Posts. Captain R.P. Anderson R.A.M.C. proceeded for duty to M.C.9/12 2/7 West Riding	R.G.W
-do-	12/9/17		Nothing to Report.	R.G.W
-do-	14/9/17		A.D.M.S. 62 Division visited the Camp.	R.G.W
-do-	15/9/17		Nothing to Report.	R.G.W
-do-	16/9/17		Nothing to Report.	R.G.W
-do-	17/9/17		Nothing to Report.	R.G.W
-do-	18/9/17		Captain P.H. Rawson M.C. transferred to 2/5 K.O.Y.L.I. as M.O. in charge	R.G.W
-do-	19/9/17		Tested A.D.S. and Collecting Post.	R.G.W
-do-	19/9/17		First Lieutenant A.P. GROSSMAN M.O.R.C. U.S.A reported for duty.	R.G.W
-do-	20/9/17		A.D.M.S. 62nd Division visited the Camp	R.G.W
-do-	21/9/17		Nothing to report	R.G.W
-do-	22/9/17		Nothing to report	R.G.W
-do-	23/9/17		Nothing to report	R.G.W
-do	24/9/17		Nothing to report.	R.G.W

Army Form C. 2118.

WAR DIARY
or
INTELLIGENCE SUMMARY.
2/3rd West Riding Field Ambulance
(Erase heading not required.)

Sheet - 1/1

Place	Date	Hour	Summary of Events and Information	Remarks and references to Appendices
FAVREUIL	25/9/17		A.D.M.S. 62nd Division visited the Camp.	RJW
-do-	26/9/17		Nothing to Report.	RJW
-do-	27/9/17		Nothing to Report	RJW
-do-	28/9/17		Nothing to Report	RJW
-do-	29/9/17		A.D.M.S. 162nd Division visited the Camp. Captain T.C. Young R.A.M.C. S.R. proceeded for temporary duty at M.D.S. 310 Brigade R.F.A.: Captain B. Wigglesworth R.A.M.C. evacuated to 29 Casualty Clearing Station suffering from Contusion of leg - right.	RJW
-do-	30/9/17		Visited the A.D.S.	RJW

RJW Thomson
LIEUT. COLONEL R.A.M.O.
COMDG. 2/3rd, WEST RIDING FIELD AMBULANCE

CONFIDENTIAL ORIGINAL Vol 10

147/2499

WAR DIARY

of

1/3rd WEST RIDING FIELD AMBULANCE

OCTOBER, 1917. VOLUME X

COMMITTEE FOR THE
MEDICAL HISTORY OF THE WAR
Date -8 DEC. 1917

"MEDICAL"

Army Form C. 2118.

WAR DIARY
or
INTELLIGENCE SUMMARY.

2/3 West Riding Field Ambulance
October 1917

(Erase heading not required.)

Instructions regarding War Diaries and Intelligence Summaries are contained in F. S. Regs., Part II. and the Staff Manual respectively. Title pages will be prepared in manuscript.

Place	Date	Hour	Summary of Events and Information	Remarks and references to Appendices
FAVREUIL	1/10/17		Nothing to Report	BJW
- do -	2/10/17		Nothing to Report	BJW
- do -	3/10/17		Nothing to Report	BJW
- do -	4/10/17		Lieutenant J.B.C. BROCKWELL R.A.M.C. T.C. reported for duty with the Field Ambulance	BJW
- do -	5/10/17		A.D.M.S. 62nd Division visited the Camp	BJW
- do -	6/10/17		Captain F. WIGGLESWORTH R.A.M.C. rejoined Unit from C.C.S.	BJW
- do -	7/10/17		Tested the A.D.S. Collecting Post	BJW
- do -	8/10/17		Tested Sub of Tent Camp at ECHELLES	BJW
- do -	9/10/17		1 Officer and 40 other ranks of 142nd Field Ambulance reported to learn the working of the line	BJW
- do -	10/10/17		1 Officer and 1 Tent Sub Division reported to take over the Main Dressing Station	BJW
			Advance Party of One Officer and 12 other Ranks proceeded to New Camp Site at LECHELLE	BJW

WAR DIARY

INTELLIGENCE SUMMARY. 2/3 West Riding Field Ambulance

October 1917 Sheet 11

Army Form C. 2118.

Place	Date	Hour	Summary of Events and Information	Remarks and references to Appendices
FAVREUIL	11/10/17		All posts in the forward area and the Main Dressing Station handed over to 142 Field Ambulance. Relief in the forward area completed by 6.0 a.m., the whole relief of Unit completed by 11.0 a.m. Scheme of Evacuation in operation whilst working the Right Sector of the line is attached herewith. The unit complete moved by road to ECHELLE and occupied the tented Camp S.16 at P.25.c.24-57. Erection of Huts started.	appendix I OCJW
ECHELLE	12/10/17			
-do-	13/10/17		Lieutenant J.R.C. BROCKWELL R.A.M.C. T.C. proceeded for duty to No 29. C.C.S. on the instructions of A.D.M.S. 62 Division. Lieutenant BROCKWELL is taken off the strength of the Unit from this date.	OCJW
-do-	14/10/17		A.D.M.S. 62 Division visited the Camp. D.D.M.S. IV Corps visited the Camp. R.A.+ Q.M.G. IV Corps visited the Camp.	OCJW OCJW

Army Form C. 2118.

October 1917
Sheet No. 11

WAR DIARY
or
INTELLIGENCE SUMMARY

(Erase heading not required.)

2/3 West Riding Field Ambulance

Instructions regarding War Diaries and Intelligence Summaries are contained in F. S. Regs., Part II. and the Staff Manual respectively. Title pages will be prepared in manuscript.

Place	Date	Hour	Summary of Events and Information	Remarks and references to Appendices
ECHELLE	15/10/17		Captain J.C. Young, R.A.M.C. 310th R.F.A.: Under Section 183 (2) of the Army Act, and powers delegated by the Army Commander, the VI Corps Commander has reduced No. 406236 Staff Sergeant Ingall H. to the rank of Corporal for inefficiency.	AJW
-do-	16/10/17		Nothing to Report	AJW
-do-	17/10/17		Nothing to Report	AJW
-do-	18/10/17		Nothing to Report	AJW
-do-	19/10/17		Nothing to Report	AJW
-do-	20/10/17		Nothing to Report	AJW
-do-	21/10/17		Nothing to Report	AJW
-do-	22/10/17		Nothing to Report	AJW
-do-	23/10/17		Nothing to Report	AJW
-do-	24/10/17		First Lieutenant A.A. Grossman, M.O.R.C., U.S.A. proceeded to 312 Brigade R.F.A. for temporary duty	AJW

WAR DIARY
or
INTELLIGENCE SUMMARY.

2/3 West Riding Field Ambulance

Army Form C. 2118.

October 1917
Sheet IV

Place	Date	Hour	Summary of Events and Information	Remarks and references to Appendices
ECHELLE	25/10/17		Nothing to Report	Rgw
-do-	26/10/17		Nothing to Report. 62nd Division "warning order" to move received	Rgw
-do-	27/10/17		Nothing to Report.	Rgw
-do-	28/10/17			Rgw
-do-	29/10/17		Unit moved by road with 187th Infantry Brigade. Occupied Billets at A.29.b.2.8. (GOMIECOURT.) Sheet 57.C.	Rgw
GOMIECOURT.	30/10/17		Unit moved with 187th Infantry Brigade by road from GOMIECOURT to BERNEVILLE and occupied billets. Headquarters of Unit at the MAIRIE BERNEVILLE. Map Reference Q.6.d.9.5. Sheet 57. C. Sqw	Rgw
BERNEVILLE	31/10/17		Captain W.A. Coats D.S.O. and Captain K.G. HAIG. R.A.M.C. reported for duty with the Field Ambulance.	Rgw

R.J.Williamson
LIEUT. COLONEL R.A.M.C.
COMMDG. 2/3rd. WEST RIDING FIELD AMBULANCE

SCHEME OF EVACUATION FROM RIGHT SECTOR.

COMBINED and LEFT R.A.P. (C 5.a.9.0.)	RIGHT R.A.P. (C 11.c.7.9.)	DISPOSAL OF PERSONNEL.
		Combined and Left R.A.P. 8 Bearers.
		Right R.A.P. 4 Bearers.

From which wounded are carried by bearers to

COLLECTING POST (Noreuil) (C 10.c.7.8.)

Collecting Post. Noreuil.
1 N.C.O.
4 Bearers.
1 Cook.
1 Dresser.
Working Party --- 3
Water Duty ------ 4

From which evacuated by

Light Railway (C 15.b.5.8.) through C 15 & C 20. to	Wheeled Stretchers to C.15.a.9.8. thence by 1. Wheeled Stretchers 2. Ford Car to

Loading Post (C 15.a.9.8.)
4 Bearers.

ADVANCED DRESSING STATION. (C 20.d.2.5.)

Advanced Dressing Station
1 Medical Officer
1 N.C.O.
12 Bearers.
2 Dressers
2 Clerks.
1 Batman.

By Daimler Cars to

MAIN DRESSING STATION. (Favreuil) (H 16.d.9.5.)

:MAP REFERENCE: :SHEET 57C:

R.G. Williamson
LIEUTENANT COLONEL R.A.M.C.T.
COMMANDING 2/3rd WEST RIDING FIELD AMBULANCE.

[Stamp: ORDERLY ROOM, October, 1917, 2/3RD WEST RIDING FIELD AMBULANCE]

MEDICAL.

CONFIDENTIAL — ORIGINAL

War Diary

of

2/3 West Riding Field Ambulance

Volume XI November 1917

COMMITTEE FOR THE
MEDICAL HISTORY OF THE WAR
Date 17 JAN. 1918

MEDICAL

Army Form C. 2118.

WAR DIARY
or
INTELLIGENCE SUMMARY.

2/3 West Riding Field Ambulance
November 1917   Sheet 1

(Erase heading not required.)

Place	Date	Hour	Summary of Events and Information	Remarks and references to Appendices
BERNEVILLE	1/11/17		Captain R.P. ANDERSON, R.A.M.C.(T) — Detached as M.O/c 2/7th West Riding Regiment — taken off the Strength on establishment of Medicine officers being completed	Appx
- Do -	2/11/17		Nothing to report.	Appx
- Do -	3/11/17		Nothing to report.	Appx
- Do -	4/11/17		Nothing to Report	Appx
- Do -	5/11/17		Captain J. M. BENSON. R.A.M.C.T. detailed for temporary duty as M.O. i/c 2/5. K.O.Y.L.I.	Appx
- Do -	6/11/17		Nothing to Report.	Appx
- Do -	7/11/17		Nothing to Report.	Appx
- Do -	8/11/17		Nothing to Report.	Appx
- Do -	9/11/17		Nothing to Report.	Appx
- Do -	10/11/17		Nothing to Report.	Appx
- Do -	11/11/17		Visited the line in front of RYAULCOURT and all posts with the D.D.M.S. 62nd Division	Appx
- Do -	12/11/17		Proceeded with 185th Infantry Brigade by road	Appx

Army Form C. 2118.

WAR DIARY
or
INTELLIGENCE SUMMARY.

2/3 West Riding Field Ambulance

November 1917.

SHEET 11

Place	Date	Hour	Summary of Events and Information	Remarks and references to Appendices
BERNEVILLE	12/11/17		to GOMIECOURT occupying buildings previously used	RfW
GOMIECOURT	13/11/17		Left Gomiecourt with 185th Infantry Brigade by road to ECHELLE. Captain J.C. YOUNG, Captain W.P. COATS and 10 Other Ranks proceeded as Advance Party to RUYAULCOURT.	RfW
ECHELLE	14/11/17		Marching to Report.	RfW
- Do -	15/11/17		Nothing to Report.	RfW
- Do -	16/11/17		Left Echelle with 185th Infantry Brigade and proceeded to RUYAULCOURT. By road. Headquarters of Unit P.10.a.8.4 57.C.	RfW
RUYAULCOURT	17/11/17 6 P.M.		3 R.A.P's and 1 Wagon Post taken over from 108/2 Field Ambulance.	RfW
- Do -	18/11/17		P.D.M.S. 62 Division visited Headquarters and Walking Wounded Post - P 18.d.2.1 - 57.C.	RfW
- Do -	19/11/17		R.A.M.C. personnel sent into the line to the R.A.P's at J.3b.d.9.b, Q.2.c.3.3., Q.3.c.7.5. Walking Wounded Post at P.18.d.5.1 and Wagon Post at P.12.b.53.- 57.C. taken over.	RfW

WAR DIARY or INTELLIGENCE SUMMARY

Army Form C. 2118.

2/3 West Riding Field Ambulance November 1917 SHEET 111

Place	Date	Hour	Summary of Events and Information	Remarks and references to Appendices
Actue Secteur	9/11/17	5 PM	Captain KENWORTHY R.A.M.C and Two Bearer Sub Divisions of 1/2 West Riding Field Ambulance reported for duty in the front area. 8 Squads of these were attached to Regimental Medical Officers - 2 Squads to each also 8 Squads of Bearers - 2/3 West Riding Field Ambulance were attached to Regimental Medical Officers - 2 Squads to each. Captain T.C. Young Lieutenant Grosvenor one tent and one Bearer Sub division were posted to the Right R.A.P. at Q.3.C.7.5. Captain F. WIGGLESWORTH R.A.M.C. and Captain T.H. KENWORTHY R.A.M.C. one tent Sub division 2/3 West Riding Field Ambulance and one Bearer Sub division of 1/2 West Riding Field Ambulance posted to Central R.A.P. at Q.2.C.3.3.	
MAP 51e				

Army Form C. 2118.

2/3 West Riding Field Ambulance
November 1917 - Sheet IV

WAR DIARY
or
INTELLIGENCE SUMMARY.
(Erase heading not required.)

Instructions regarding War Diaries and Intelligence Summaries are contained in F. S. Regs., Part II. and the Staff Manual respectively. Title pages will be prepared in manuscript.

Place	Date	Hour	Summary of Events and Information	Remarks and references to Appendices
Achiet Operations MAP 51Q	19/11/17		Captain W.A. COATS, Bruce. Captain H. PICKLES RAMC. one tent sub-division 2/3 W.R.F. Ambulance and one Bearer Sub-Division 2/1 W.R.F. Ambulance were posted to left R.A.P. at J.36.d.9.6., Captain H.W. ROBINSON RAMC.T. and Captain J.W. WAYTE RAMC.T. and 20. R.A.M.C. personnel were posted at W.W Post P.18.d.5.1. Advanced R.A.P.'s at Q.4.c.2.8. K.32.b.9.6. and K.32.a.20.05 were established in which a supply of stretchers, blankets and dressings were placed.	
	20/11/17	6.30 am	The Division attacked and at the line surveyed forward the 3. R.A.P's became collecting posts. Evacuation from the Right and Centre being to the A.D.S. (51st Division) at P.14.d.2.6. by hand carriage and wheeled stretcher.	

WAR DIARY
or
INTELLIGENCE SUMMARY.

Army Form C. 2118.

1/3 West Riding Field Ambulance
November 1917 — Sheet V

Place	Date	Hour	Summary of Events and Information	Remarks and references to Appendices
Active Operations Mouffet 51c	20/11/17		Walking Wounded directed down through the Wood to P.18.d.5.1 from there by Busses and Decauville to B/S. (1/2 W.R. F.Amb.) Evacuation of Stretcher cases from A.D.S. (P.14.d.2.6) by M.A.C. cars to C.C.S. at YPRES where 4 clerks of 1/3 W.R.F. Amb. were posted to record admissions. Evacuation now from left - T.36.d.9.6. - by Field Ambulance Cars which were posted in Sunken road at T.36.c.6.8. to Main Dressing Station at RUYAULCOURT (51st Division) New Walking wounded post through P.18.d.5.1. up to date 1083.	
		10 am	Result. Sub Division asked for, from 2/1 W.R.F.Amb.; Captains POPE and BLACKBURN and two Bearer Sub Divisions 8 2/1 W.R. F. Ambulance reported at P.18.d.51. later in the day. BGW

WAR DIARY or INTELLIGENCE SUMMARY

2/3 West Riding Field Ambulance
November 1917

Place	Date	Hour	Summary of Events and Information	Remarks and references to Appendices
Hebuterne Mab 51C	29/11/17	11 P.M.	Captain POPE instructed to move up to HAVRINCOURT & establish an Advanced Dressing Station at Collecting Post and get in touch with Captain KENWORTHY who had been instructed to move forward. Bearers and get in touch with Regimental Medical Officers of 186th Brigade. Captain JC Young was instructed to send Lieutenant PA GROSSMAN and Bearers forward to establish a Relay Post between Captain POPE and Captain KENWORTHY.	
	2/11/17		Captain JC Young and Bearers moved to HAVRINCOURT establishing posts at K.16.d.9.7 and got in touch with Captain KENWORTHY who had established at K.S.d.9. Later in the day Captain Young moved forward to join Captain Kenworthy and a post was established on north side of GRAVEL PIT. Ogso	

Army Form C. 2118.

WAR DIARY
or
INTELLIGENCE SUMMARY.
(Erase heading not required.)

2/3 West Riding Field Ambulance

November

SHEET VII

Place	Date	Hour	Summary of Events and Information	Remarks and references to Appendices
Jecture	21/11/17		About K.6.a.19 Bearers were pushed forward to keep in touch with 186th Brigade. Captain BLACKBURN pushed north six squads 2/1 13R.F. Ambulances sent to Q.2.c.3.3. During afternoon evacuation by G.S. Cars and Horsed Ambulances was established between K.32.b.9.8. and Q.2.c.3.3 and from Q.2.c.3.3 and back to A.D.S. by Field Ambulance Cars and Relays of Wheeled Stretchers from HAVRINCOURT to K.32.b.9.8.	
Map 52 c	22/11/17	2.0 am	Captain Blackburn and Six Squads sent forward from Q.2.c.33. to HAVRINCOURT.	
		7.30 am	Bearers were pushed forward and party from Q.2.c.33 were pushed forward to assist Captain [Blackburn] going in front of HAVRINCOURT. A line of evacuation was established by Rifle Regt.	

WAR DIARY or INTELLIGENCE SUMMARY

Army Form C. 2118.

1/3 West Riding Field Ambulance
November 1917 Sheet VIII

Place	Date	Hour	Summary of Events and Information	Remarks and references to Appendices
Active Operations Maps 51b	22/11/17		Posts from GRAINCOURT to the Watering Post at HERMIES (36th Division) by relay of the Canal. Captain PICKLES Returns all four Dismounted Cars, having sent to half north this concentration. Captain W.A. COATS and party left R.A.P. at T.36.d.9.6 proceeded to G.2.C.33 and then journeyed to GRAINCOURT. Lieutenant Colonel LISTER 2/1 W.R. & Amb proceeded to HERMIES to assist in that line of evacuation. Orders received for relief of Divisions on the line. Motorcyclists sent to Capt. and WIGGLESWORTH YOUNG and POPE to proceed on relief to RUYAULCOURT.	
	23/11/17		62nd Division was relieved in the line. Rank & File Personnel 2/1 and 2/1 W.R. F Ambulances were returned to their units at Regt. reported.	

Army Form C. 2118.

2/3 West Riding Field Ambulance Sheet 1
November 1917

WAR DIARY
or
INTELLIGENCE SUMMARY.
(Erase heading not required.)

Place	Date	Hour	Summary of Events and Information	Remarks and references to Appendices
Ruyaucourt	24/11/17		Nothing to Report	
Fekue	25/11/17		Moved from RUYAULCOURT to TRESCAULT Q.4.c.8.3. and Sent Route Reconnoitre into the line to take over from the 110th Division Line of Evacuation from R.A.Ps to A.D.S. Graincourt by Road. Bearer post to A.D.S. Graincourt open order 6 A.D.S. Graincourt Divisions open FLESQUIERES by horsed Ambulances Hence by M.A.C. Cars and sick Ambulance Cars A.C.C.S. YTRES Walking wounded by Am Cars at K.4.d.31 K.10.a.od.40.6 K.9.d.6.0 to A.D.S. HAVRINCOURT thence by Ambulance Cars to YTRES Horsed Ambulances run along road mentioned above from Graincourt to Havrincourt Disposition of R.A.M.C. Personnel as follows:-	Appx

WAR DIARY
or
INTELLIGENCE SUMMARY.

Army Form C. 2118.

1/3 West Riding Field Ambulance
November 1917 Sheet

Place	Date	Hour	Summary of Events and Information	Remarks and references to Appendices
Achiet le Grand Map 51c	28/11/17		M.D.S. GRAINCOURT Lieut Colonel Parry and Lieut But Division Captain M.C. and Lieutenant A.H. GROSSMAN there being Sub Division and to which Stretcher 1/3 W.R. Ambulance is attached to M.D.S. Graincourt got in touch with R.M.O's of 187th Brigade and 187th Brigade detailing 2 Stretcher to each R.M.O. Captains P & B BLACKBURN and 3 Bearer Squads and 1 Lieut Sub Divisions proceeded to M.D.S. Havrincourt. Captain BEKKES and one and half Bearer Sub Division and Captain KENWORTHY and two Bearer Sub Divisions of 1 W.R. Field Ambulance proceeded to A.D.S. GRAINCOURT to assist in duty Captain J.C. Young	AgW

WAR DIARY or INTELLIGENCE SUMMARY

Army Form C. 2118.

1/3 West Riding Field Ambulance
November 1917
Sheet 1

Place	Date	Hour	Summary of Events and Information	Remarks and references to Appendices
Advance Operations Map 5C	20/11/17		Captain F. WIGGLESWORTH and one Tent Sub-Division - 2/3 W.R.Funt proceeded to A.D.S. FLESQUIERES relieving 2/2 O/C 2 Field Ambulance. Captain H.W. ROBINSON, R.A.M.C. and 4 W.C.O.S reported at the Walking Wounded Post-TRESCAULT to assist the officer in charge - 4 Field Ambulance. Captain Young, A.D.S. GRAINCOURT K.56.S.4. sent forward (Bearer) to ANNEUX-CHAPEL and commenced to evacuate from Dressing Post at K.12.a.4.8 by Horsed Ambulance to FLESQUIERES and also by Field Ambulance along the GRAINCOURT - HAVRINCOURT Road from R.4 & 6.5. to A.D.S. HAVRINCOURT. During the day GRAINCOURT was heavily Shelled and at night Lieutenant Young Rush to evacuate Huns to A.D.S. RBW	

WAR DIARY or INTELLIGENCE SUMMARY

Army Form C. 2118.

13/West Riding
Field Ambulance
November 1917 Sheet XII

Place	Date	Hour	Summary of Events and Information	Remarks and references to Appendices
Retuse Operations Map 57/19	26/11		and establish a collecting post at the BRICK KILNS about K.15.b.6.8.	
	27/11		Evacuation to be through a collecting post at the Sugar Factory at E.29.a.8.9. South of BOURLON WOOD through by Buses to K.4.d.6.5 from there by field Ambulance cars to BRICK KILN Collecting Post and so on to HAVRINCOURT E.D.S. from there by M.A.C. cars to YPRES Walking wounded to be transferred to TRESCAULT from thence sent by DECAUVILLE and Buses to YPRES. During the afternoon Capt. A.W. KENWORTHY 20th R.W.S.I.K. Regiment took over K.12.a.48 in sub-sector a new and established a Relay Post at F.26.a.1.6.	page 13 ogu ogn

WAR DIARY or INTELLIGENCE SUMMARY

Army Form C. 2118.

1/3 West Riding Field Ambulance
November 1917 Sheet XIII

Place	Date	Hour	Summary of Events and Information	Remarks and references to Appendices
Active Service	27/11/17		Cases were carried from R.A.P at F.13.c.8.5 to Relay Post at F.26. to Loading Post at K.12.c.5.8 from there by Horse Ambulance to R.D.S (FLESQUIERES) at as an alternative from Relay Post at F.26. by German Trolley line to K.M.d.9.6 and then by Horse Ambulance to FLESQUIERES P.D.S. thence by M.A.C. to YTRES.	
	28/11/17		No alterations were made in the above arrangements	
	29/11/17		67 Division relieved in the line by 47th Division R.A.M.C. Personnel relieved by Regs	
	30/11/17	11.30 a.m	Unit moved to LEBUCQUIERE 135.2.3.4	Regn

Lieutenant Colonel RAMC
O.C 1/3 West Riding Field Ambulance

"MEDICAL"

CONFIDENTIAL 6

ORIGINAL

COMMITTEE FOR THE
MEDICAL HISTORY OF THE WAR
Date −1 FEB. 1918

WAR DIARY
OF
2/3 WEST RIDING FIELD AMBULANCE

1st TO 31st
DECEMBER 1917

VOLUME XII

"MEDICAL"

Army Form C. 2118.

WAR DIARY
or
INTELLIGENCE SUMMARY.
(Erase heading not required.)

2/3 West Riding Field Ambulance

December 1917   Sheet No. 1

Place	Date	Hour	Summary of Events and Information	Remarks and references to Appendices
LEBUCQUIERE	1/12/17		Nothing to report.	
- Do -	2/12/17		Nothing to report.	
- Do -	3/12/17		Entrained with 187th Infantry Brigade from LEBUCQUIERE; detrained at FREMICOURT.	
BLAIREVILLE	4/12/17		Marched by road with 187th Infantry Brigade to BLAIREVILLE.	
DUISANS	5/12/17		Marched by road with 187th Infantry Brigade to DUISANS.	
BETHONSART	6/12/17		Marched by road with 187th Infantry Brigade to BETHONSART.	
- Do -	7/12/17		Nothing to report.	
- Do -	8/12/17		Nothing to report.	
- Do -	9/12/17		Marched by road with 187th Infantry Brigade to HESDIGNEUL.	
HESDIGNEUL	10/12/17		Nothing to report.	
- Do -	11/12/17		Nothing to report.	
- Do -	12/12/17		Nothing to report.	
- Do -	13/12/17		Nothing to report.	
- Do -	14/12/17		Nothing to report.	
- Do -	15/12/17		Nothing to report.	

Army Form C. 2118.

WAR DIARY
or
INTELLIGENCE SUMMARY.
(Erase heading not required.)

2/3 West Riding Field Ambulance
December 1917 — Sheet 11

Place	Date	Hour	Summary of Events and Information	Remarks and references to Appendices
HESDIGNEUL	16/12/17		Captain W. R. COATS R.A.M.C. taken off the Strength of Field Ambulance on posting to 2/5 K.O.Y.L.I. as Medical officer i/c.	
			Military Medals awarded to 405068 Corporal LAKE N.H. and 405142 Private BARKER S.W. by IV Corps Commander for gallantry during operations which commenced on November 28th 1917.	See Appx
- Do -	17/12/17		Nothing to Report.	
- Do -	18/12/17		Moved by road with 187th Brigade from HESDIGNEUL to HERMIN. Unit in Billets Headquarters P.22.d.3.- 36.5.	See Appx
HERMIN	19/12/17		Nothing to Report	See Appx
do	20/12/17		Visit of A.D.M.S. 62 Division	See Appx
do	21/12/17		Nothing to report.	See Appx
do	22/12/17		Captain T. M. BENSON evacuated to 42 CCS	See Appx
do	23/12/17		Nothing to report.	See Appx
do	24/12/17		Captain F. WIGGLESWORTH reports to 2/1 York & Lancs. for temporary duty	See Appx

Army Form C. 2118.

WAR DIARY
or
INTELLIGENCE SUMMARY.
(Erase heading not required.)

2/3 West Riding Field Ambulance
December 1917 — Sect III

Place	Date	Hour	Summary of Events and Information	Remarks and references to Appendices
HERMIN	24/12/17		CAPTAIN T.M.BENSON evacuated from 42 CCS to BASE by Ambulance Train No 22 and taken off the strength accordingly	R/w
do	25/12/17		Nothing to report.	R/w
do	26/12/17		Nothing to report.	R/w
do	27/12/17		CAPTAIN R.D. FITZGERALD (R.A.M.C. T.C.) reported for duty and taken on the strength accordingly	R/w
do	28/12/17		CAPTAIN N. PURCELL R.A.M.C. (T.C) and CAPTAIN R.E.S. PRINGLE-PATTISON R.A.M.C (T.C) reported for duty and were taken on the strength accordingly.	R/w R/w
do	29/12/17		CAPT. W. SNEDDON mentioned in despatches	R/w
			Nothing to report.	R/w
do	30/12/17		Nothing to report.	R/w
do	31/12/17		CAPTAIN N. PURCELL proceeded to XIII Corps Rest Station for temporary duty.	R/w
			MILITARY CROSS awarded to CAPT. J.C. YOUNG R.A.M.C (R)	R/w
			DISTINGUISHED CONDUCT MEDAL awarded to No 405204 Staff Sgt TORRIW	R/w

R.G. Williamson
LIEUT. COLONEL R.A.M.C
COMMDG. 2/3rd. WEST RIDING FIELD AMBULANCE

CONFIDENTIAL

ORIGINAL 95/13

WAR DIARY

OF

2/3RD WEST RIDING FIELD AMBULANCE

JANUARY 1918.

VOLUME XIII

COMMITTEE FOR THE
MEDICAL HISTORY
Date -4 MAR.1918

MEDICAL

Army Form C. 2118.

WAR DIARY ORIGINAL 2/3 West Riding Field Ambulance
~~INTELLIGENCE SUMMARY.~~
January 1918 SHEET No 1.
(Erase heading not required.)

Instructions regarding War Diaries and Intelligence Summaries are contained in F. S. Regs., Part II. and the Staff Manual respectively. Title pages will be prepared in manuscript.

Place	Date	Hour	Summary of Events and Information	Remarks and references to Appendices
HERMIN	1/1/18		Nothing to Report	
do	2/1/18		Visited Headquarters 2/3rd London Field Ambulance - ANZIN - and arranged taking over in the forward area.	Rgw
-do-	3/1/18		Nothing to Report	Rgw
-do-	4/1/18		Nothing to Report	Rgw
-do-	5/1/18		Captain R.O. Fitzgerald. R.A.M.C. Captain A.E.S. Pringle-Pattison. and fifty other ranks reported to O.C. 2/3 London Field Ambulance to take over posts in forward area	Rgw
-do-	6/1/18		No. 405051 Acting Staff Sergeant. Patkison. H. and No. 46986 Sergeant. Wagnall. W. awarded the Meritorious Service Medal (vide Supplement to London Gazette January 1st 1918)	Rgw
-do-	7/1/18		Captain J.C. Young. M.C. R.A.M.C. and Sunull Advance Party take over Field Ambulance Camp. ANZIN. from 2/3 London Field Ambulance.	Rgw

WAR DIARY ORIGINAL
or
INTELLIGENCE SUMMARY.

Army Form C. 2118.

2/3 West Riding Field Ambulance
Sheet 2.

January 1918.

Place	Date	Hour	Summary of Events and Information	Remarks and references to Appendices
HERMIN	8/1/18		Unit moved by road from HERMIN to ANZIN St AUBIN.	Ryw
ANZIN ST AUBIN	9/1/18		Visited A.D.S. and all posts in Left Sub-Sector of line. Captain J.C. Young M.C. R.A.M.C. and 405057 Staff Sergeant Phillips? proceeded to First Army R.A.M.C. School to attend course of instruction	Ryw
- Do -	10/1/18		Visited A.D.S. and all posts in Right Sub Sector of line with A.D.M.S. 62 Division	Ryw
- Do -	11/1/18		A.D.V.S. XIII th Corps inspected Lines of transport	Ryw
- Do -	12/1/18		Bearer Sub Division arrived from 2/2 West Riding Field Ambulance	Ryw
- Do -	13/1/18		Nothing to Report	Ryw
- Do -	14/1/18		Nothing to Report.	Ryw
- Do -	15/1/18		Nothing to Report.	Ryw
- Do -	16/1/18		D.D.M.S. XIII th Corps and A.D.M.S. 62 Division Visited A.D.S. (GUN PITS) Right Sub Sector: 12 men reported from 2/2 W.R. G.O.C. 62ND (W.R.) Division and G.O.C. 185th Brigade Visited A.D.S. (RAILWAY CUTTING) Left Sub Sector.	Ryw

WAR DIARY ORIGINAL

Army Form C. 2118.

INTELLIGENCE SUMMARY. 2/3 West Riding Field Ambulance Sheet 3
January 1918

Place	Date	Hour	Summary of Events and Information	Remarks and references to Appendices
ANZIN St AUBIN	17/1/18		Nothing to Report	
	18/1/18		Visited A.D.S. Left Sub Sector with A.D.M.S. 62 Division	Rgw
-Do-	19/1/18		Nothing to Report.	Rgw
-Do-	20/1/18		Visited Right Sub Sector of line. Captain J.C. Young M.C. R.A.M.C. and 405051 Staff Sgt. Pattison returned from First Army R.A.M.C. School	Rgw
-Do-	21/1/18		Captain A.E.S. PRINGLE-PATTISON R.A.M.C. transferred to 2/4 York and Lancs. Regt as Medical officer in charge. No 405051 Staff Sergeant Pattison A. proceeded to First Army R.A.M.C. School as Instructor. No. 405216. Pte Shelton G. and No. 1676. Pte Goodge J. wounded in action.	Rgw
-Do-	22/1/18		Visited A.D.S (under construction) at Point Du Jour-Right Sub-Sector. 12 Bearers report from 2/2 W.R.F. Amb. Rgw	Rgw
-Do-	23/1/18		Captain F. WIGGLESWORTH R.a.m.C.T and No. 401341. Sergeant Raper E.B. proceeded to First Army R.a.m.C. School to attend course of Instruction. Captain W. SHARRARD. R.A.M.C.T. reported	Rgw

T2134. Wt. W708—776. 500000. 4/16. Sir J. C. & S.

WAR DIARY ORIGINAL

Army Form C. 2118.

INTELLIGENCE SUMMARY. 2/3 West Riding Field Ambulance
Sheet 4.
January 1918

(Erase heading not required.)

Instructions regarding War Diaries and Intelligence Summaries are contained in F.S. Regs., Part II. and the Staff Manual respectively. Title pages will be prepared in manuscript.

Place	Date	Hour	Summary of Events and Information	Remarks and references to Appendices
Anzin St	23/1/18	(contd)	for duty from 2/4 York Lancs Regt.	Offrs Regts
Aubin	24/1/18		Nothing to Report	
Do	25/1/18		Visited A.D.S. - Left Sub Sector - Railway Cutting. D.D.M.S. XIII Corps and A.D.M.S. 62 Division visited A.D.S. Railway Cutting	
Do	26/1/18		Nothing to Report	
Do	27/1/18		Officer arrived from 2/2 W.R. Field Ambulance for duty in forward area. Captain W. Sheppard R.A.M.C. proceeded to 2/2 W.R. Field Ambulance for temporary duty. Captain H.B. Pope R.A.M.C 2/1st W.R. Field Ambulance attached for duty as Officer in charge A.D.S. Gun Pits	Offrs Offrs
-Do-	28/1/18		Visited A.D.S. Gun Pits and New Relay Post (Light Cases). G.O.C. 62 Divsion inspected Transport. Camp Captain R.D. Fitzgerald R.A.M.C. proceeded to VII Corps for duty, and is taken off the Strength.	Offrs
-Do	29/1/18		A.D.M.S. 1/62 Division visited A.D.S Railway Cutting	Offrs Offrs

WAR DIARY

~~INTELLIGENCE SUMMARY~~

ORIGINAL Sheet 5 2/3 West Riding Field Ambulance
January 1918.

Army Form C. 2118.

Instructions regarding War Diaries and Intelligence Summaries are contained in F.S. Regs., Part II. and the Staff Manual respectively. Title pages will be prepared in manuscript.

Place	Date	Hour	Summary of Events and Information	Remarks and references to Appendices
ANZIN ST AUBIN	30/1/18		Visited A.D.S. Railway Cutting (Left-Sub Sector) DDMS. XIII Corps and ADMS. 62 Division visited A.D.S. Ryn Gun Pits. (Right-Sub-Sector) Nothing to Report.	
	31/1/18		Nothing to report.	

O.C. Williamson
Lieutenant-Colonel R.A.M.C.
Commanding 2/3 West Riding Field Ambulance
2/3 West Riding Field Ambulance

MEDICAL

CONFIDENTIAL

ORIGINAL

WAR DIARY
OF
2/1 WEST RIDING FIELD AMBULANCE

VOLUME XIV

FROM FEB. 1ST 1918
TO FEB. 28TH 1918

COMMITTEE FOR THE
MEDICAL HISTORY OF THE WAR
Date -8 APR. 1918

MEDICAL
SHEET 1.
Army Form C. 2118.

2/3 WEST RIDING FIELD AMBULANCE. FEB. 1918

WAR DIARY
INTELLIGENCE SUMMARY.
(Erase heading not required.)

ORIGINAL

Place	Date	Hour	Summary of Events and Information	Remarks and references to Appendices
Auzin St Aulair	1/2/18		Visited A.D.S. (Gunpits) and relay posts of the Right Subsector	R.W
"	2/2/18		Captain F. Wigglesworth. S. Sergeant Pattinson and Sergt. Rapn returned from First Army R.A.M.C School.	R.W
"	3/2/18		Captain N. Purcell today transferred to 93rd F. Ambulance in exchange for Captain T.W. Frew who is taken on the strength of this unit. Capt. H.B. Pope returned to 2/1 W.R.F Ambulance from A.D.S (Gunpits), being relieved by Capt F. Wigglesworth.	R.W R.W
"	4/2/18		Captain W. Sharard rejoined this unit from 2/1 W.R.F Ambulance A.D.M.S. 62nd Division visited the A.D.S. and forward posts of the Right Sector	R.W R.W
"	5/2/18		Nothing to report.	R.W
"	6/2/18		Visited the Right Sector. Sergt. Gregson reported to the First Army R.A.M.C School. The D.A.D's.M.S 56 and 62 Divisions visited the A.D.S. Railway & Gunpits	

SHEET 2

2/3 WEST RIDING FIELD AMBULANCE FEB 1918

ORIGINAL

WAR DIARY
INTELLIGENCE SUMMARY
(Erase heading not required.)

Army Form C. 2118.

Instructions regarding War Diaries and Intelligence Summaries are contained in F.S. Regs., Part II. and the Staff Manual respectively. Title pages will be prepared in manuscript.

Place	Date	Hour	Summary of Events and Information	Remarks and references to Appendices
Anzin St Aubin	7/2/18		Capt. A.E.S. Pringle-Pattison reported from the 2/4 York and Lancs and was taken on the strength of this unit from 7/2/18. He reported to O.C. 5 K.O.Y.L.I. for temporary duty as R.M.O. Capt. W. Sneddon attended a conference at the office of D.D.M.S. XIII Corps	SR/W SR/W
"	8/2/18		Visited the A.D.S. Railway Cutting. Capt. W. Sharrard with 6 O.R. proceeded as advance party to Houvelin. An advance party of 2 officers and 30 O.R. of 2/2 London Field Ambulance arrived to take over the line. A.D.M.S. 62 Division visited the A.D.S. Railway Cutting. 50 o.Rhs & tanks of the 2/2 W.R.F. Ambulance at Habarcq to this unit for duty in the line were returned to the 2/2 W.R.F. Ambulance.	SR/W SR/W SR/W
"	9/2/18		A plan of the scheme of evacuation, as carried out by this unit on this front since 7/1/18, were drawn up.	Attached as Appendix I SR/W

SHEET 3
Army Form C. 2118.

WAR DIARY
or
INTELLIGENCE SUMMARY.
(Erase heading not required.)

2/3 WEST RIDING FIELD AMBULANCE
ORIGINAL
FEB 1918

Place	Date	Hour	Summary of Events and Information	Remarks and references to Appendices
Anzin St Aubin	9/2/18		A progress report was submitted to the ADMS 62 Division regarding the work done in the forward area during the tour of duty of this unit and the work done on the camp site at Anzin, together with a plan of the ante-rooms proposed to be provided.	Attached as Appendix II
"	10/2/18		All posts in the forward area were handed over to the 2/1 London Field Ambulance.	RJW
Houvelin	11/2/18		Lieut Colonel F.G. WILLIAMSON M.C. proceeded on thirty days leave. The unit proceeded to Houvelin under the orders of 185 Infantry Brigade, marching to Maroeuil where the men were entrained. After detraining at Tingues, the remainder of the journey was completed by route march through Chelers and Frevillers to the transport under the command of Captain Fugglesworth and the whole journey by road. Lieutenant A.A. GROSSMAN M.O. R.C.U.S. proceeded for temporary duty to 2/4 Duke of Wellingtons Regiment,	RJW FGW

SHEET 4.
Army Form C. 2118.

1/3 West Riding
Field Ambulance Feb 1918

ORIGINAL

WAR DIARY

INTELLIGENCE SUMMARY.

(Erase heading not required.)

Place	Date	Hour	Summary of Events and Information	Remarks and references to Appendices
Hauclin	11/2/18		Captain W. SHARRARD RAMC was evacuated sick to 42 C.C Stay	
"	12/2/18		nothing to report	
"	13/2/18		nothing to report.	
"	14/2/18		Captain W.J. FREW RAMC proceeded to XIII Corps Rest Station (2/1 London F. Ambulance) for temporary duty.	
"	15/2/18		nothing to report	
"	16/2/18		nothing to report.	
"	17/2/18		CAPTAIN T.E. YOUNG RAMC SR was evacuated to 42 C.C.S.	
"	18/2/18		nothing to report.	
"	19/2/18		nothing to report.	
"	20/2/18		CAPTAIN F WIGGLESWORTH attended a conference held by the D.D.M.S XIII Corps.	
"	21/2/18		L'/ & Q.M H M BROWNE attended a lecture on Food Economy at HOUDAIN	
"	22/2/18		nothing to report.	
"	23/2/18		CAPTAIN T.E. YOUNG RAMC S.R was taken off the strength, CAPTAIN J.W.R.	

Sheet 5.
Army Form C. 2118.

2/3 WEST RIDING FIELD AMBULANCE
ORIGINAL FEB 1918

WAR DIARY
INTELLIGENCE SUMMARY.
(Erase heading not required.)

Place	Date	Hour	Summary of Events and Information	Remarks and references to Appendices
Houvelin	23/2/18		FREW was admitted to 42 C.C.S.	tst
	24/2/18		nothing to report.	tst
	25/2/18		nothing to report.	tst
	26/2/18		nothing to report.	tst
	27/2/18		LIEUTENANT A.A. CROSSMAN M.O. R.E. U.S.A reported for duty from the 2/4 Duke of Wellings 16's Reg.	tst
	28/2/18		A Syllabus of the programme of training as carried out since February 13th was proposed and as attached.	Appendix III

Hhigglesworth Capt RAMC
tr O.C. 2/3rd W.R.Ft Amb

Scheme Of Evacuation.

(Corrected to 8/2/18)

APPENDIX 7

RIGHT SUB-SECTOR.

Two R.A.P's.   THAMES R.A.P.   TOWY R.A.P.
(B.30.a.8.9.)   (B.30.c.5.2.)

Three Relay Posts.   GAVRELIE RELAY   TOWY RELAY   NEW RELAY.
(B.30.a.4.4.)   (H.5.b.1.9.)   (H.4.b.9.2.)
- unfinished -

Advanced Dressing Station.   GUN PITS.
(H.4.c.5.5.)

NEW ADVANCED DRESSING STATION.   POINT DU JOUR.
(H.9.a.2.8.)

Evacuation takes place during daylight by trench from both R.A.P's to the Relay Posts and from the Relay Posts partly by trench and partly by road and track.
The route for the last half of the Right Sector is from the R.A.P. down MARINE TRENCH to the point where THAMES TRENCH cuts MARINE TRENCH (B.30.a.5.6.) then by THAMES TRENCH to a point (B.29.c.6.4.) where a duckboard track behind some camouflage crosses to the GAVRELIE ROAD (B.29.c.8.2.). At this place a wheeled stretcher is used down the road to the entrance of the trench leading into the A.D.S. If the road is being shelled the bearers continue the duckboard track over the road behind the camouflage to TOWY TRENCH. This track is about 200 yards long and ends in cutting TOWY TRENCH at the TOWY RELAY POST (H.5.b.1.9.) Then on, down TOWY TRENCH, to the entrance to TOWY TRENCH into the sunken road by NEW RELAY (H.4.b.9.2.) Then over the track to the GUN PITS A.D.S. (H.4.c.5.5.). From A.D.S. by stretcher along GAVRELIE ROAD to POINT DU JOUR, (H.9.a.2.8.) At night a car waits at the trench by A.D.S.
From the right half of the right sector evacuation takes place by trench as far as TOWY RELAY (H.5.b.1.9.) and then either by duckboard track to the GAVRELIE ROAD (B.29.c.8.2.) where a wheeled stretcher is kept, or by TOWY TRENCH as explained above.

THAMES R.A.P. Is a large Bosche dugout with two entrances facing towards the Bosche, capable of holding and storing wounded during heavy shelling preventing evacuation for a short while.

GAVRELIE RELAY. Is an English dug out with 10 feet of head cover, capable of holding twenty stretcher cases and walking wounded.

TOWY R.A.P. Is a deep English dugout with three entrances, capable of holding twenty stretcher cases and walking wounded, and is approached by a gradual-sloped passage. Also has a de-gassing chamber.

TOWY RELAY. Has accomodation for 4 stretcher cases. Its entrance faces towards the Bosche lines and it is merely splinter-proof.

NEW RELAY. Is at present being made. It is a small dugout with 20 feet of head cover and two entrances cut in the side of the sunken road; it is well strutted with Bosche mining frames. The dugout is being cut out of hard chalk. From its position in the sunken road and in the event of an advance could easily be made into an Advanced Dressing Station by building additional rooms all with exits into the sunken road. The size of the chamber is 9 feet by 20 feet and can be extended if necessary.

GUN PITS A.D.S. Is composed of two Bosche Gun Pits with concrete roofs supported by iron girders and has about 18 inches of soil on top. The gun pits are connected by an underground passage out of which lead a store house, cook house, officers quarters and mens quarters. There is accomodation for storing 32 stretcher cases.
POINT DU JOUR. There is a large chamber with two exits facing the Bosche line at this point; this chamber is being connected up with another Bosche dug out with a view to having an A.D.S. here which will accomodate at least 30 stretcher cases.

LEFT SUB SECTOR.

A.   Medical Accomodation.

R.A.P's of the two Battalions in the front line are situated as follows:-

Right R.A.P.   (Viscount Street.) - B.24.a.7.7.

Left R.A.P.   (South Duke Street) - B.18.c.8.6.

The left R.A.P. is being enlarged and when completed each R.A.P. will be capable of accomodating about six stretcher cases awaiting evacuation.
The R.A.P. of the Battalion in support is in RED LINE (B.23.a.1.8)
The R.A.P. of the Battalion in reserve is in the RAILWAY CUTTING (B.27.a.5.8.)

RELAY POST No.1.   (B.17.c.6.1.) Junction of OUSE ALLEY and MACHINE GUN TRENCH.

RELAY POST No.2.   (B.16.c.7.5.) OUSE ALLEY.   cases.
Each relay post could accomodate, if necessary, 4 or 5 stretcher

A. D. S. RAILWAY CUTTING. (B.27a.4.7.) This consists of a dressing room, a collecting station for upwards of eight stretchers cases, a cook house, officers quarters, sleeping quarters for six men and a small store house.   The accomodation, however, is unsatisfactory and more accomodation is being built near.

R.A.M.C. RAILWAY SIDING.   (B.26.b.8.4.)   Two Red Crossed covered trucks are stationed here each capable of carrying 8 stretcher cases and in addition a few standing cases.

A. D. S. - CHANTECLER.   This is held by R.A.M.C. personnel but is not at present opened as a Dressing Station.   It is much larger than the A.D.S. RAILWAY CUTTING.

B.   ROUTES AND METHODS OF EVACUATION.

Hand Carry.   From front line R.A.P's down OUSE ALLEY to RELAY POST No.1., from RELAY POST No.1 to RELAY POST No.2., continuing down OUSE ALLEY, and on by the same route through the tunnel under railway - B.21.a.7.9.   Thence along a duckboard track to the left under cover of the west bank of the railway embankment to a point - B.21.c.8.8. where the duckboard track strikes the BAILLEUL ROAD. A trench runs between the points B.21.c.7.7. and B.21.c.7.4. thus terminating in the RAILWAY CUTTING.   This is the completely covered route for DAYLIGHT evacuation, but it is long and tedious and is only suitable for the evacuation of urgent cases during heavy shelling in the neighbourhood of BAILLEUL VILLAGE.
There are two other routes from RELAY POST No.2. to the A.D.S. The first is by striking across the open from RELAY POST No.2. to the RAILWAY LINE at a point about B.16.c.5.2. and then by following the railway line right up to the A.D.S.   The line forks twice on this journey and each time the bearers take the left fork.   This route of evacuation is the one most frequently employed although technically, the railway line is not supposed to be used in day time.   The second route is by road between the points B.16.c.1.3. and B.21.b.3.0.   A wheeled stretcher can be employed along this road.   Squads returning from No. 1. RELAY POST to the R.A.P. are supposed to return via TYNE ALLEY and not via OUSE ALLEY which is meant for down traffic only.

Push Trolley.   Stretcher cases can be evacuated by this means from the R.A.P's to the A.D.S.   The left R.A.P. drains into the OPPY LINE, while the right R.A.P. drains into the TYNE LINE.   Both lines conveniently pass about 100 yards from RELAY POST No.1., link up with eachother and pass within 200 yards of RELAY POST No.2. and thence to A.D.S.

Push trolley - continued.

From R.A.P's to RELAY POST No.1. This method of evacuation can only be employed at night time and from there onwards on days of poor visibility. However, some cases could be stored during the day at the R.A.P's in order to take advantage of this means of evacuation.

TRAIN SERVICE.

Sick are sometimes evacuated by the return ration train from the line at night. This service, under pressure of cases, might by agreement with the railway authorities be extended by sending the Red Crossed covered trucks up to the RED LINE at night time and collecting cases from RELAY POST No.1. Normally the train service is restricted to carrying cases from the A.D.S. RAILWAY CUTTING to M.D.S. St. CATHERINE via CHANTECLER.

AMBULANCE CARS.

Cases can, if need be, be evacuated by car from the A.D.S., the loading point is MAISON DE LA COTE (B.20.d.7.1) which is about 400 yards carry from the A.D.S. This is the farthest point forward which a car is supposed to proceed in daylight. In case of difficulty with the railway line, or pressure of cases, the car should proceed on a misty day or at night time from MAISON DE LA COTE through BAILLEUL VILLAGE to the cross-roads (B.22.d.8.95). This place is only about 600 yards from RELAY POST No.1. and would form a very convenient emergency spot near to which cases could be brought and dumped for car evacuation.

AMBULANCE PERSONNEL.	Officers.	N.C.O's.	Men.	
LEFT R.A.P.	-	-	4	
RIGHT R.A.P.	-	-	4	
Relay Post No.1	-	1	6	x
Relay Post No.2	-	-	5	
A.D.S. RAILWAY CUTTING	2	2	10	
	2	3	29.	

It will be observed that the above represents a skeleton staff only.
x This includes two runners.
Since the A.D.S. does not posses any telephone communication two men are kept as messengers at RELAY POST No.1., since this would be the first relay post to receive news of heavy casualties in the line.
There is a short cut from RELAY POST No.1. to A.D.S. as follows:-
A track near the Realy Post to a point B.23.a.4.4. - where the track crosses the RED LINE - and thence by a straight track (sunken) to B.27.b.7.6. From this point another track bearing slightly to the right runs to B.27.a.4.8. at which place there is a path leading down the embankment to the A.D.S. A message by this route takes only twenty-five minutes.

TRAMWAYS.

The officer in charge Tramways at ROCLINCOURT (Captain Campbell, H.L.I. attached R.E.) has given consent for the two covered Ambulance trucks in the RAILWAY CUTTING to proceed at night on demand being made to the Sergeant-Major, R.E. to a point near the RED LINE where the OPPY PUSH BRANCH commences at approximately B.22.b.9.7. They will be drawn by tractor. These trucks should not be requisitioned until there are at least eight cases from No. 1. RELAY POST for removal.

PgWilliamson
Lieutenant Colonel, R.A.M.C.T.
Feb.1918.   Commanding 2/3 West Riding Field Ambulance.

APPENDIX 11   2/3rd West Riding Field Ambulance.

PROGRESS OF WORK ON CAMP SITE AT ANZIN.

1. The manure traverses at the ends of the horse standings are now practically completed.
2. The traverse at each end of the row of seven Nissen Huts has been completed and work is progressing on the traverses between the huts.   A plan of proposed scheme of protection has been drawn up to be handed over to the incoming unit.
(Copy of plan - Appendix 2.)

PROGRESS OF WORK IN FORWARD AREA.   - Map 51.B. -

1. Three elephant huts, 18 feet long by 8 feet wide, have been erected at B.27.a.6.9.   Two have been lined with wood and sandbagged outside, the third is not yet completed.   The middle one is now racked for twelve stretchers.   The Three Huts are joined together by a covered gangway.
2. Work has been carried on at the new Relay Post - H.4.b.9.4. A 20 feet by 9 feet chamber with 20 feet of cover and two entrances - one sloped for stretchers - is in course of construction.   The chamber is almost completed and will be racked for 12 stretchers.
3. Work has been continued at the POINT-DU-JOUR dugout - H.9.a.2.8. The tunnel between the large chamber and the old German dug out has been completed.   Officers quarters, off the tunnel, are in process of construction.   A Cook House has been made in the entrance to the large dugout.   Latrine made. Thirty stretcher cases can be accomodated at this dugout.

                                        Lieutenant Colonel, R.A.M.C.(T)
                        Commanding 2/3rd West Riding Field Ambulance.

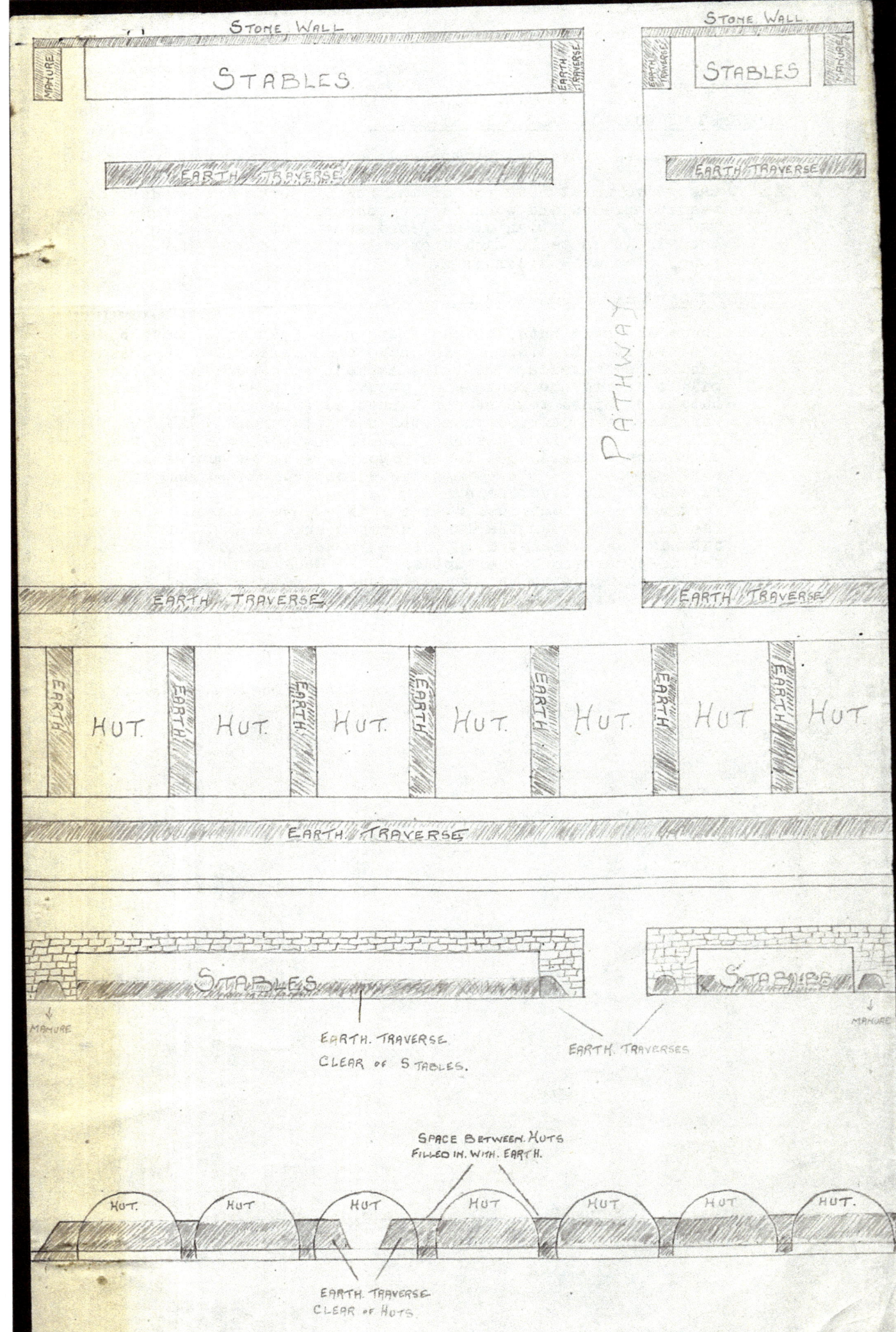

APPENDIX 3.

PROGRAMME OF TRAINING.
2/3 West Riding Field Ambulance.

Date	9. to 9-30.	9.30 to 10-30	10-30 to 11-30	11-30 to 12-30		2.p.m.
Wednesday Feb. 13th	Foot rubbing.	Physical Drill	Resuscitement & Treatment of Shock and application of Thomas Splint.	Stretcher Drill in Small Box Respirators.	Dinner	Methods of carrying Stretchers.
Thursday Feb. 14th	Foot rubbing	Physical Drill	--- R o u t e M a r c h ---		Dinner	Application of Thomas Splint.
Friday Feb. 15th	Foot rubbing	Physical Drill	Squad Drill & Saluting Drill		Dinner	Lecture: Economy in War time.
Saturday Feb. 16th	Foot rubbing	---	Commanding Officer's Inspection		Dinner	Football
Sunday Feb. 17th	Foot rubbing	Medical Inspection	------ Church Parades ------		Dinner	
Monday Feb. 18th	Batning Parades, followed by Foot Rubbing and Fatigue Duties.				Dinner	Kit Inspection.
Tuesday Feb. 19th	Foot rubbing	Physical Drill	--- R o u t e M a r c h ---		Dinner	Inspection of Small Box Respirators and Gas Drill
Wednesday Feb. 20th	Foot rubbing	Physical Drill	Full marching order parade. Company Drill.		Dinner	Application of Thomas Splint.
Thursday Feb. 21st	Foot rubbing	Physical Drill	Squad & stretcher drill in S. B. R's	Extended order drill	Dinner	Lecture: Arrest of Haemorrhage.

	9? to 9.30.	9.30 to 10.30	10.30 to 11.30	11.30 to 12.30		2 p.m.
Friday, Feb. 22nd.	Foot rubbing	Physical Drill	------ Route March ------		Dinner	Application of Thomas Splint
Saturday Feb. 23rd	Foot rubbing	Physical Drill	Full Marching Order Parade. (Including Transport) Commanding Officer's Inspection. Pay Parade ------ 12 Noon.		Dinner	Football.
Sunday Feb. 24th	Foot rubbing	Medical Inspection and Inspection of Identity discs	------ Church Parades ------		Dinner	------
Monday Feb. 25th	Foot rubbing	Physical Drill	Company Drill	Saluting Drill	Dinner	Stretcher Drill
Tuesday Feb. 26th	Bathing Parades, followed by Foot Rubbing and Fatigue Duties.				Dinner	Route March.
Wednesday Feb. 27th	Foot rubbing	Physical Drill	Application of Thomas Splint.		Dinner	Route March
Thursday Feb. 28th.	Foot rubbing	Physical Drill	------ Route March ------		Dinner	Kit Inspection.

20th February, 1918.

Hughworth Capt RAMC
for Lieutenant Colonel, R.A.M.C.(T).
Commanding 2/3 West Riding Field Ambulance.

MEDICAL

6
CONFIDENTIAL
May 1918
ORIGINAL
(140/349) Vol. 15

WAR DIARY
OF
2/3 WEST RIDING FIELD AMBULANCE

MARCH 1918

VOLUME XV

COMMITTEE FOR THE
MEDICAL HISTORY OF THE WAR
Date 12 MAY 1918

MEDICAL

Army Form C. 2118.

WAR DIARY or INTELLIGENCE SUMMARY.

ORIGINAL

MARCH 1918 2/3 WEST RIDING FIELD AMBULANCE
SHEET 1.

(Erase heading not required.)

Place	Date	Hour	Summary of Events and Information	Remarks and references to Appendices
Houvelin	1/3/18		Lieutenant A.A. GROSSMAN M.O.R.C. U.S.A. and advance party proceeded to Anzin to take over from the 95th Field Ambulance.	
"	2/3/18		The unit proceeded by road to Anzin, taking over from the 95th Field Ambulance. Hafer Chateau G.8.a.s.2. 51/B.	
Anzin	3/3/18		Daily routine of Hospital duties, fatigues, the work of 95th Field Ambulance in auto bomb protection continued.	
"	4/3/18		Daily routine — nothing to report.	
	5/3/18		Daily routine — nothing to report.	
	6/3/18		Daily routine — nothing to report.	
	7/3/18		One tent subdivision (two officers) reported to 2/1 West Riding Field Ambulance (III Corps Rest Station) Aubigny for duty. Sergt. Tiffin, King and Corporal Soyer proceeded on course to XIII Corps M.R.C. Floringhem. Lieut Quartermaster H.M. BROWNE attended a lecture on the "Food Situation" at XIII Corps.	
	8/3/18		Daily routine — nothing to report.	

WAR DIARY
INTELLIGENCE SUMMARY

MARCH 1918
2/3 WEST RIDING FIELD AMBULANCE
SHEET 2

Army Form C. 2118.

ORIGINAL

Place	Date	Hour	Summary of Events and Information	Remarks and references to Appendices
Angus	9/3/18		A.D.M.S. 62nd Division visited the Camp.	
"	10/3/18		Lieut. A.A. GROSSMAN M.O.R.C. U.S.A. proceeded to the 62 Divisional Machine Gun Battalion as M.O. in charge	
"	11/3/18		Daily routine - nothing to report.	
"	12/3/18		One N.C.O. and 11 men reported to the 2/2 West Riding Field Ambulance as working party for Commandant's Horse lines	
"	13/3/18		One N.C.O and 9 men, two N.C.Os and 18 reported to the 2/2 West Riding Field Ambulance, the former party for work at Divisional Headquarters, the latter for work at A.D.S. Long Wood under orders of the M.O i/c 83rd Brigade R.G.A.	
"	14/3/18		Daily routine - nothing to report	
"	15/3/18		Captain F. WIGGLESWORTH R.A.M.C. attended a conference at D.D.M.S office. Lieut. Col. P.G. WILLIAMSON R.A.M.C returned from leave	
"	16/3/18		1 N.C.O and 8 men reported to O.C. 2/2 W.R.F.Amb. as working party	
"	17/3/18		Captain F. WIGGLESWORTH reported to O.C. 2/2 WEST RIDING FIELD AMBULANCE for temporary duty. Three Daimler cars were sent to O.C.	

WAR DIARY or INTELLIGENCE SUMMARY.

Army Form C. 2118.

2/3 WEST RIDING FIELD AMBULANCE
MARCH 1918. SHEET 3
ORIGINAL

Place	Date	Hour	Summary of Events and Information	Remarks and references to Appendices
Curgin	17/3/18		2/2 W. Riding Field Ambulance to assist in evacuation. CAPTAINS T.S. ROWLANDS and C.F. GRAVES R.A.M.C. affiliated to this unit for duty.	RGW
"	18/3/18		Nothing to report.	RGW
"	19/3/18		CAPTAIN F. WIGGLESWORTH returned from duty with the 2/2 WEST RIDING FIELD AMBULANCE	RGW
"	20/3/18		Visited the left sector of the forward area of the 56 "Divisional Front"	RGW
"	21/3/18		2 Officers with all available bearers and 3 Daimler cars were held in readiness to support the 2/2 WEST RIDING FIELD AMBULANCE	RGW
"	22/3/18		Nothing to report.	RGW
"	23/3/18		All working parties from 2/2 W.R.F. Ambce. and the tent sub-division with 2/1 W.R.F. Ambce. were returned to the unit.	RGW
ARRAS	24/3/18		The unit moved into ARRAS with 187 Inf. Brigade taking over the HOSPICE de VIEILLARDS. Arrangements were made with O.C. 45 FIELD AMBULANCE to evacuate wounded from 187 Inf Brigade through his posts and 24 bearers were held in readiness to be attached two squads to each battalion.	RGW

Army Form C. 2118.

WAR DIARY
—or—
INTELLIGENCE SUMMARY.
(Erase heading not required.)

2/3 WEST RIDING FIELD AMBULANCE SHEET IV
MARCH 1918
ORIGINAL

Place	Date	Hour	Summary of Events and Information	Remarks and references to Appendices
ARRAS.	25/3/18	3 a.m	orders were received to proceed with 185 Brigade via AGNY to AYETTE and BUCQUOY. The unit arrived at BUCQUOY at 5 P.M and encamped on the BUCQUOY-LES ESSARTS Road two kilos from BUCQUOY.	
		6.30 P.M	CAPTAINS WIGGLESWORTH and SHARRARD with two bearer subdivisions were sent to establish a line of evacuation from 185 BRIGADE who were holding a line in front of LOGEAST WOOD. Relay posts were established on the BUCQUOY – ACHIET LE PETIT Road with a car control post on the west of BUCQUOY. Cases were evacuated by wheel stretcher to a collecting post outside BUCQUOY on the ACHIET LE PETIT Road thence by car to HANNESCAMPS.	
BUCQUOY	26/3/18		Information being received that the infantry were retiring, the unit moved via HANNESCAMPS, FONQUEVILLERS, SOUASTRE and headquarters were finally established at MAGH at HUMBERCAMP.	
			The collecting post was moved from BUCQUOY to HANNESCAMP and relay posts were established on the road from BUCQUOY to HANNESCAMP cases being evacuated by car and horse ambulance to the MDS at HUMBERCAMP.	

WAR DIARY
or
INTELLIGENCE SUMMARY.

Army Form C. 2118.

2/3 WEST RIDING FIELD AMBULANCE

MARCH 1918 SHEET V

ORIGINAL

Place	Date	Hour	Summary of Events and Information	Remarks and references to Appendices
HUMBERCAMP	27/3/18.		A line of evacuation was established through GOMMECOURT and FONQUEVILLERS from 187 INF. BRIGADE. Captain FREW was sent to establish a collecting post in GOMMECOURT with four squads and a bearer post for the loading of cars was established in FONQUEVILLERS	
		8.30 p.m.	The collecting post was moved back to GOMMECOURT WOOD on the road side.	RJW
"	28/3/18.		The bearer post at FONQUEVILLERS was converted into an advanced dressing station, Captain WIGGLESWORTH being sent up to take charge with Captain GRAVES and four more squads. Cars were sent towards HEBUTERNE to evacuate wounded from the 4th Australian Brigade on our right.	RJW
"	29/3/18.		Captain ROWLANDS and all bearers of the 2/3 W.R.F. Amb. were transferred from the left to the right. Captain GRAVES, 1 N.C.O and 40 men were sent to evacuate wounded from the Australian Brigade and the following posts were established, relay posts at K.9.B.39 and K.3.c.9.9. Collecting post at E.27.a.9.5.D	RJW

Army Form C. 2118.

WAR DIARY
or
INTELLIGENCE SUMMARY.

2/3 WEST RIDING FIELD AMBULANCE SHEET VI
MARCH 1918
ORIGINAL

(Erase heading not required.)

Place	Date	Hour	Summary of Events and Information	Remarks and references to Appendices
HUMBERCAMP	30/3/18		CAPTAIN GRAVES went forward to an Australian Battalion to replace a casualty, CAPTAIN SHARRARD taking his place at the collecting post. Went to St Leger, Grignour to look for a field ambulance site. RyW	
HUMBERCAMP.	31/3/18.	5 p.m	Visited FONQUEVILLERS — Evacuation proceeding satisfactorily. CAPT SHARRARD having been relieved returned to HQ Evacuation proceeding satisfactorily. RyW RyWilkinson Lieutenant Colonel Ranyer Commanding 2/3 West Riding Field Ambulance	

MEDICAL

CONFIDENTIAL ORIGINAL / 96/6

WAR DIARY
OF
2/3 WEST RIDING FIELD AMBULANCE

140/2900

VOLUME XV

APRIL 1918

COMMITTEE FOR THE
MEDICAL HISTORY OF THE WAR
Date 6 JUN 1918

MEDICAL

Army Form C. 2118.

WAR DIARY
or
INTELLIGENCE SUMMARY.

2/3 West Riding Field Ambulance Sheet 1
April 1918

ORIGINAL

Place	Date	Hour	Summary of Events and Information	Remarks and references to Appendices
HUMBERCAMP	1/4/18		All posts in the forward area were handed over to the 50th Field Ambulance. The personnel on relief proceeded to billets in COIGNEUX.	
MARIEUX	2/4/18		The camp site at HUMBERCAMP was handed over to the 50th Field Ambulance and the unit proceeded via Coigneux to rest billets in the aerodrome at MARIEUX.	
"	3/4/18		The ADMS visited the camp.	
"	4/4/18		Attended a conference of Field Ambulance Commanders at the ADMS office.	
"	5/4/18		Visited the 1/3 East Lancashire Field Ambulance at BIENVILLERS with a view to taking over.	
"	6/4/18		CAPTAIN FREW 1 NCO 24 bearers reported to O.C. 1/3 East Lancashire F.A. BIENVILLERS as advance party. Two squads (8 bearers) were attached to the Medical Officers of the 8th West Yorks, 2/5 West Yorks, 2/7 West Yorks. Of CAPTAIN FREW'S party one man was detailed to each R.A.P. to act as guide	

WAR DIARY
or
INTELLIGENCE SUMMARY

Army Form C. 2118.

1/3 W. & B. Riding April 1918
Field Ambulance
Sheet 2

ORIGINAL

Place	Date	Hour	Summary of Events and Information	Remarks and references to Appendices
MARIEUX	7/4/18		Major WIGGLESWORTH, two NCOs and two Squads were sent forward to continue the relief. Major Wigglesworth's duty being to act as liaison officer to the Three Infantry Brigade Headquarters.	
			Captains BLACKBURN and PICKLES, two N.C.O's and 40 men of the 2/1st W R F Amber were sent to relieve the 1/3rd EAST LANCS F Amber in the Regt section of the Divisional front and collect wounded from 186 Inf BRIGADE.	
			The remainder of the unit moved to HENU. The transport lines and Quartermasters stores of the East Lancs Field Amber were taken over. The Headquarters went forward to take over the ADS and Headquarters of the 1/3rd EAST LANCS F.A. at BIENVILLERS	
			The relief of all posts and the ADS was completed by midnight.	
			The scheme of evacuation is shown in attached appendix.	See Appendix I
BIENVILLERS	8/4/18		Visited Collecting and relay posts in the forward area.	
			A new relay post was established halfway between HANNESCAMPS and ESSARTS, also a FORD CAR post was established 1000yds in front of HANNESCAMPS, loading post.	
	9/4/18		Evacuation proceeded satisfactorily. 58 men were relieved in the forward area.	

Army Form C. 2118.

2/3 West Riding
APRIL 1918
Field Ambulance
Sheet 3

WAR DIARY
or
INTELLIGENCE SUMMARY.
(Erase heading not required.)

ORIGINAL

Instructions regarding War Diaries and Intelligence Summaries are contained in F.S. Regs., Part II. and the Staff Manual respectively. Title pages will be prepared in manuscript.

Place	Date	Hour	Summary of Events and Information	Remarks and references to Appendices
BIENVILLERS	10/4/18		Two new lines of evacuation were established avoiding the ESSARTS-HANNESCAMPS road. The System is shewn in attached Scheme of evacuation and included two loading posts, one at FONQUEVILLERS for the right sector and one at MONCHY-AU-BOIS for the left sector.	Appendix II
"	11/4/18		The ADMS visited the right sector. The collecting post at E 23 d 3.3. was moved to E 23 d 4.6. The work done on la BAYELLE Road had greatly improved it for carrying. By	
"	12/4/18		Visited MONCHY and post at F.7. a 4.5. This is a long carry and bad surface and is frequently shelled.	
"	13/4/18		MAJOR GENERAL BRAITHWAITE visited the A.D.S. at BIENVILLERS visited post in R. sector. More accommodation is being built at FONQUEVILLERS loading post. One of the two RAP's at F.22 central was moved to F.26 b 7.4. 150 Infantry reported for duty as additional bearers, 50 being accommodated at ADS BIENVILLERS, and 50 each with OC's 2/1, & 2/2 W.R. F. Ambces.	

T2134. Wt. W708—776. 50000. 4/15. Sir J.C. & S.

Army Form C. 2118.

WAR DIARY
or
INTELLIGENCE SUMMARY.
(Erase heading not required.)

2/3 West Riding Field Ambulance

APRIL 1918.

ORIGINAL

Place	Date	Hour	Summary of Events and Information	Remarks and references to Appendices
BIENVILLERS	16/4/18		A.D.M.S. visited the right sector. 50 of the attached infantry were sent forward 25 to each sector. The relief was so arranged that each squad was composed of two infantry and two R.A.M.C. bearer.	RJW
"	16/4/18		Nothing to report.	RJW
"	17/4/18		Visited posts in the left sector	RJW
"	18/4/18		Visited Right Sector	RJW
"	19/4/18		Nothing to report.	RJW
"	20/4/18		Nothing to report.	RJW
"	21/4/18		Visited left sector	RJW
"	22/4/18		O.C. 49th Field Ambulance visited the A.D.S. Bienvillers to arrange relief. 1 officer and 26 other ranks of the 49 F.A. reported to commence the relief of the right sector	RJW
"	23/4/18		A second party of the 49th Field Ambulance reported to continue the relief Major Sneddon, Lieutenant Cameron and one rank subaltern were sent to the IV Corps Rest Station advance party to the mill, Authie to take over the relief.	RJW

Army Form C. 2118.

WAR DIARY
or
INTELLIGENCE SUMMARY.
(Erase heading not required.)

2/3 West Riding Field Ambulance
APRIL 1918
ORIGINAL Sheet 5

Place	Date	Hour	Summary of Events and Information	Remarks and references to Appendices
BIENVILLERS	24/4/18		The handing over of the A.D.S. and posts in the forward area to the 49th FIELD AMBULANCE was completed. The unit moved to the nissen at AUTHIE and the taking over of IV Corps REST STATION was completed.	
AUTHIE	25/4/18		Work was commenced on the rest station. A plan of the REST STATION to attached	Appx
"	26/4/18		A.D.M.S. 62 Division visited the rest station.	Appx
"	27/4/18		D.D.M.S IV Corps visited the rest station	Appx
"	28/4/18		nothing to report.	Appx
"	29/4/18		With MAJOR WIGGLESWORTH I attended a meeting at the A.D.M.S office.	Appx
"	30/4/18		nothing to report.	Appx

R.E. Williamson LIEUT COLONEL
Commanding 2/3 West Riding Field Ambulance.

APPENDIX 1.

Evacuation of Wounded from the IVth. Corps Left Divisional Front.

First Scheme.   From 7/4/18 to 2.p.m. 10/4/18.   Map Reference. 57 D.

--------------oOo--------------

P O S T S.   Regimental Aid Posts.   E.30.a.5.6.   )
                                     F.26.c.2.9.)   RIGHT SECTOR.
                                     F.26.a.5.1.)

                                     F.22.central (2 R.A.P's) -   )
                                     F.27.b.2.9. (This is also   )   LEFT SECTOR.
                                                   a Relay Post))

                                     E.24.c.4.3.)
                                     E.30.a.5.6.)   SUPPORT.
                                     F.20.d.4.7.)

             R e l a y   P o s t s.   F.14.d.1.1.
                                      F.27.b.2.9.   - (this is also a R.A.P.)
                                      E.17.d.8.3.   - (x)

             Collecting Post.
             E S S A R T S.   E.24.b.7.2.

             Ford Car Post.   E.17.a.1.7.   - (x)

             Loading Post.
             HANNESCAMPS.   E.10.c.1.7.

             A.D.S., BIENVILLERS.   E. 2.d.5.8.

        (x) These posts were established on 8/4/18.

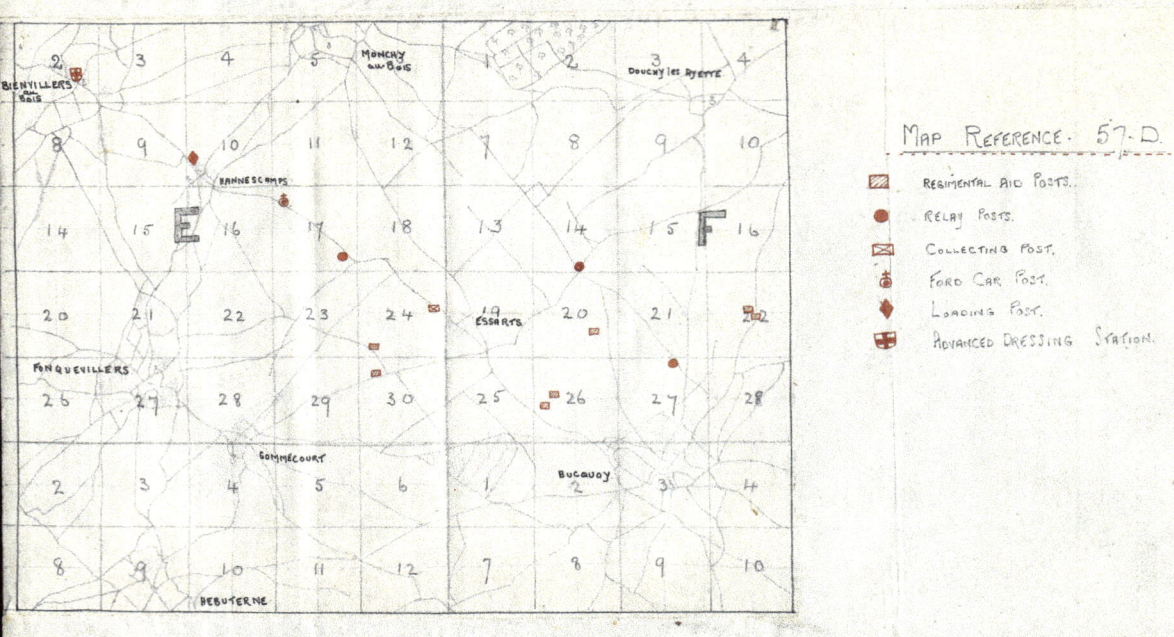

Routes of Evacuation.

FROM REGIMENTAL AID POSTS

F.26.c.2.9. F.26.a.5.1.	E.30.a.5.6. E.24.c.4.3.	F.20.d.4.7.	F.22.central (2 R.A.P's)
Evacuation by wheeled stretcher or hand carriage along BUCQUOY-ESSARTS Road to	By hand carriage to	Evacuation by hand carriage to	Evacuation by hand carriage to
		RELAY POST. F.14.d.1.1. thence by wheeled stretcher along road through F.20.a. F.19.b. to	RELAY POST. F.27.b.2.9. and on to RELAY POST F.14.d.1.1. thence by wheeled stretcher and hand carriage to

COLLECTING POST, ESSARTS.
E.24.b.7.2.

thence by wheeled stretcher
to
RELAY POST. E.17.d.8.3.

and by wheeled stretcher
to
FORD CAR POST. E.17.a.1.7.

thence by Ford Car or wheeled
stretcher to
LOADING POST, HANNESCAMPS.
E.10.c.1.7.

then in Daimler Cars to
ADVANCED DRESSING STATION, BIENVILLERS. E.2.d.5.8.

P.L. Williamson   LIEUT COLONEL
Commanding 2/3 West Riding Field Ambulance.

2/3rd WEST RIDING FIELD AMBULANCE.
No. WDXV/1
Date 30-4-18

APPENDIX I

2/3rd WEST RIDING FIELD AMBULANCE.

APPENDIX 2. Evacuation of Wounded from the IVth Corps Left Divisional Front.

Second Scheme.   From 2.p.m. 10/4/1918 to Noon 24/4/1918.   Map Reference.   57.D.

POSTS.	Regimental Aid Posts.	F.26.d.5.1. F.26.c.2.9.	) Right Sector.
		F.22.central (2 R.A.P's.)	) Left Sector.
		F.27.b.2.9. (also RELAY POST.) E.30.a.5.6. E.24.c.4.3.	) Support.
	Relay Posts.	E.30.b.6.9. E.22.d.2.5.	) Right Sector.
		F.27.b.2.9. (also R.A.P.) F.14.d.1.2. F. 7.a.4.5. (in trench) E.6. a.2.4.	) Left Sector.
	Collecting Post.	E.23.d.3.3.	) Right Sector.
	Loading Post. FONQUEVILLERS.	E.21.b.4.3.	) Right Sector.
	Loading Post. MONCHY au BOIS.	E.5.a.5.5.	) Left Sector.
	Advanced Dressing Station BIENVILLERS.	E.2.d.5.8.	

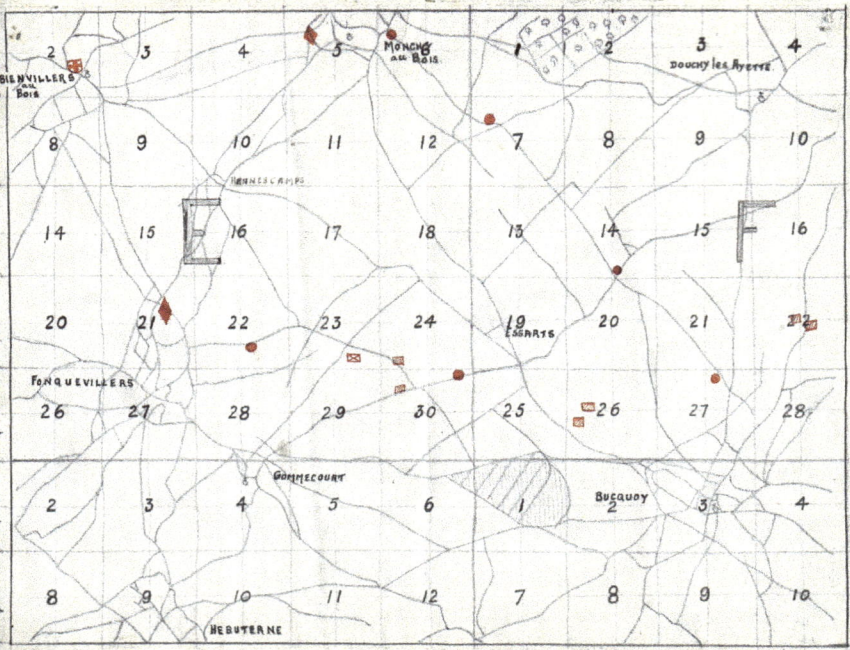

Map Reference - 57.D

▨ Regimental Aid Post.
● Relay Post
⊠ Collecting Post.
◆ Loading Post
⊕ Advanced Dressing Station.

Routes of Evacuation.

RIGHT SECTOR.

From Regimental Aid Posts.

F.26.a.5.1.   F.26.c.2.9.
  by wheeled stretcher
       to
RELAY POST. E.30.b.6.9.
  then by wheeled stretcher
  and hand carriage
       to
COLLECTING POST. E.23.d.3.3.
  then by wheeled stretcher
  or hand carriage
       to
RELAY POST. E.22.d.2.5.
  and on by wheeled stretcher
  or hand carriage
       to
LOADING POST, FONQUEVILLERS, E.21.b.4.3.
  Then by Daimler cars
       to

LEFT SECTOR.

From Regimental Aid Posts

F.22.central.   F.22.central.
  by hand carriage to
RELAY POST, F.27.b.2.9.
(this is also a R.A.P.)
  by hand carriage to
RELAY POST, F.14.d.1.2.
  then by wheeled stretcher down MONCHY ROAD
       to
RELAY POST, F.7.a.4.5.
     (in trench)
  then by hand carriage (the road here is too
  bad for wheeled stretchers)
       to
RELAY POST. E.6.a.2.4.
  and on by wheeled stretchers
       to
LOADING POST, MONCHY au BOIS, E.5.a.5.5.
  Then by Daimler cars
       to

ADVANCED DRESSING STATION, BIENVILLERS.
         E.2.d.5.8.

P.W. Williamson LIEUT COLONEL
Commanding 2/3 West Riding Field Ambulance.

APPENDIX 2

2/3RD
WEST RIDING
FIELD AMBULANCE.

(MEDICAL)

1 ORIGINAL

CONFIDENTIAL

ORIGINAL 9/8/17
140/2983

War Diary

of

2/3rd West Riding Field Ambulance

May. 1918.

Volume XVII

COMMITTEE FOR THE
MEDICAL HISTORY OF THE WAR
Date 9 JUL 1919

(MEDICAL)

WAR DIARY

INTELLIGENCE SUMMARY

Army Form C. 2118.

May, 1918.
1/3 West Riding Field Ambulance
SHEET 1

ORIGINAL

(Erase heading not required.)

Instructions regarding War Diaries and Intelligence Summaries are contained in F. S. Regs., Part II. and the Staff Manual respectively. Title pages will be prepared in manuscript.

Place	Date	Hour	Summary of Events and Information	Remarks and references to Appendices
AUTHIE	1/5/18		Construction work was continued at the Corps Rest Station — including the provision of ovens for the cook house, latrines, incinerator, repairs to the woodwork of floors, and the erection of a firescape. PLAN ATTACHED	Appendix I
"	2/5/18		routine - nothing to report.	Sgw
"	3/5/18		A.D.M.S. visited the camp	Sgw
"	4/5/18		nothing to report.	Sgw
"	5/5/18		nothing to report	Sgw
"	6/5/18		nothing to report	Sgw
"	7/5/18		nothing to report	Sgw
"	8/5/18		nothing to report	Sgw
"	9/5/18		nothing to report	Sgw
"	10/5/18		nothing to report	Sgw
"	11/5/18		nothing to report	Sgw
"	12/5/18		nothing to report.	Sgw
"	13/5/18		Twelve cases of P.U.O were admitted from 2/4 K.O.Y.L.I These cases	Sgw

WAR DIARY
INTELLIGENCE SUMMARY

Army Form C. 2118.

May 1918.
2/3 West Riding Field Ambulance.

ORIGINAL

Place	Date	Hour	Summary of Events and Information	Remarks and references to Appendices
AUTHIE	12/5/18		were selected from a total of 28, whose the occupants of two tents. The temperatures varied from 102.2 to 103.8 and they were not typical of the ordinary trench fever in the absence of skin pains. The presence of coryza and slight bronchitis. They were isolated in a separate ward.	RJW
"	13/5/18		no other development took place and the temperatures still continuing high	RJW
"	14/5/18		They were evacuated to 29. C.C.S.	RJW
"	15/5/18		I visited O.C. 50th Field Ambulance to arrange the taking over of the Field Ambulance site at PAS.	RJW
"	16/5/18		Nothing to report.	RJW
"	17/5/18	9.am	MAJOR WIGGLESWORTH and one tent subdivision proceeded to PAS to take over the hospital from 50th FIELD AMBULANCE.	RJW
		1.45pm	CAPTAIN SHARRARD with one bearer division, two cars, two wheel stretchers proceeded to report to O.C. 2/2 W.R.F. AMBULANCE at BIENVILLERS.	RJW
		"	27 bearers with 6 stretchers proceeded to report to the battalions of 187 INF.	RJW

Army Form C. 2118.

May 1918.

2/3. West Riding Field Ambulance

Sheet III

WAR DIARY
INTELLIGENCE SUMMARY.

ORIGINAL

Place	Date	Hour	Summary of Events and Information	Remarks and references to Appendices
AUTHIE	17/5/18	2pm	BRIGADE, one nurse and two squads to each MEDICAL OFFICER.	
"	18/5/18		The unit proceeded to PAS, the personnel by the road through I.10.3 and C.27, the transport by THIEVRES and FAMECHON.	ofm
PAS			A small detention hospital was established for the detention of sick, slightly wounded and NYD gas from the forward area.	ofm
"	19/5/18		Nothing to report.	ofm
"	20/5/18		CAPTAIN T.W. FREW and the remaining bearer subdivision proceeded to report to O.C. 2/2 W.R.F. Ambce. at HENU.	ofm
"	21/5/18		Nothing to report.	ofm
"	22/5/18		Nothing to report.	ofm
"	23/5/18		Nothing to report.	ofm
"	24/5/18		Nothing to report.	ofm
"	25/5/18		Nothing to report.	ofm
"	26/5/18		Nothing to report.	ofm
"	27/5/18		Nothing to report.	ofm
"	28/5/18		Nothing to report.	ofm

WAR DIARY
INTELLIGENCE SUMMARY

(Erase heading not required.)

ORIGINAL

Army Form C. 2118.

May 1918. 2/3 West Riding Field Ambulance.

Place	Date	Hour	Summary of Events and Information	Remarks and references to Appendices
P.A.S.	29/5/18		nothing to report.	
	30/5/18		nothing to report.	
	31/5/18		nothing to report.	

R.J.Williamson
LIEUT COLONEL
Commanding 2/3 West Riding Field Ambulance.

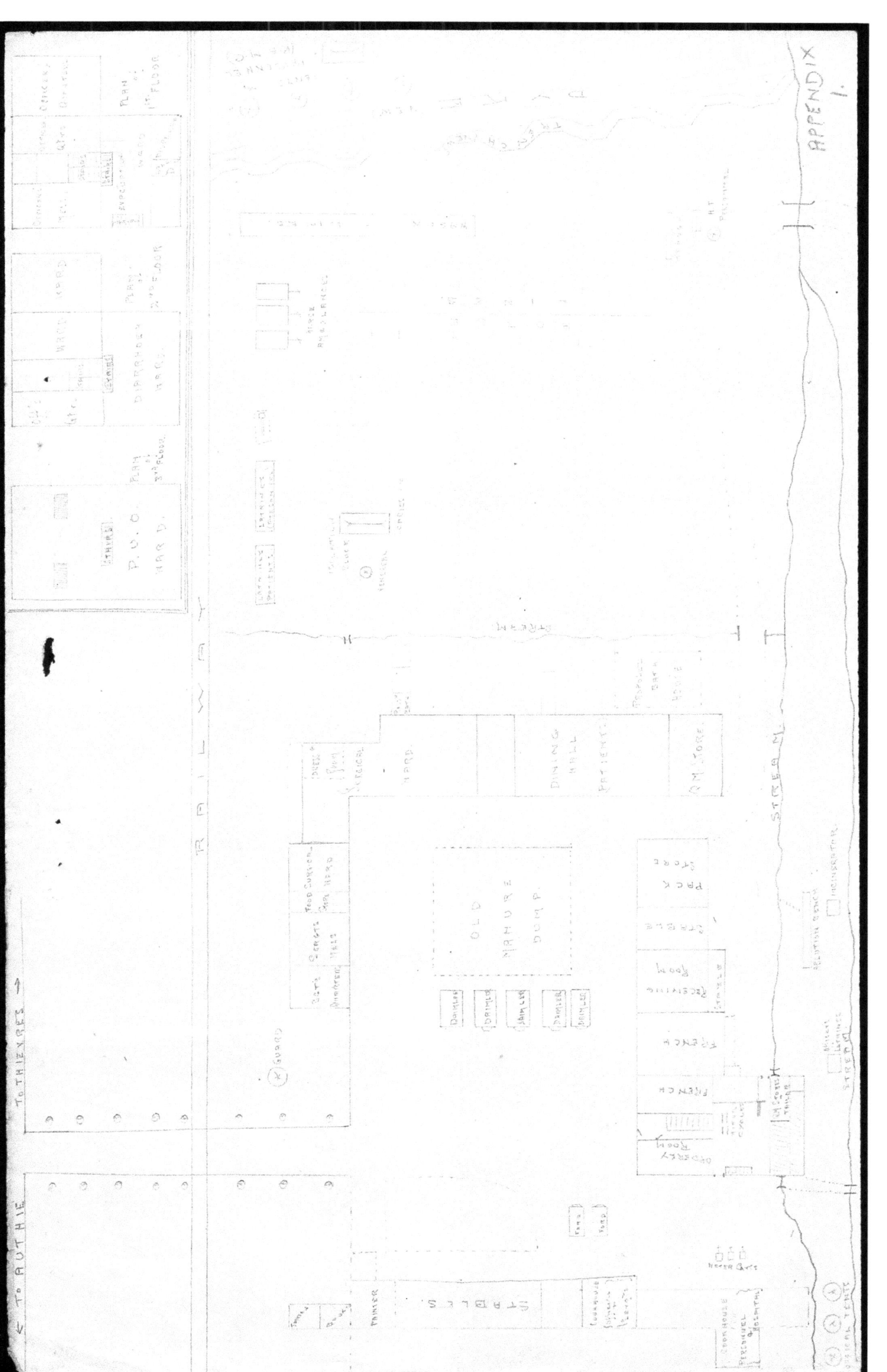

MEDICAL.

CONFIDENTIAL. ORIGINAL

June 1918

Vol 18
120/30%

WAR DIARY
of
2/3RD WEST RIDING FIELD AMBULANCE

JUNE. 1918

COMMITTEE FOR THE
MEDICAL HISTORY ...
Date 7 AUG 1918

VOLUME XVIII

2/3RD
WEST RIDING
FIELD AMBULANCE.
No...........
Date...........

MEDICAL.
Army Form C. 2118.

2/3rd WEST RIDING FIELD AMBULANCE
JUNE, 1918   SHEET I
ORIGINAL

WAR DIARY

INTELLIGENCE SUMMARY.
(Erase heading not required.)

Instructions regarding War Diaries and Intelligence Summaries are contained in F.S. Regs., Part II. and the Staff Manual respectively. Title pages will be prepared in manuscript.

Place	Date	Hour	Summary of Events and Information	Remarks and references to Appendices
P.A.S.	1/6/18		Nothing to report.—	Regt
	2/6/18		Nothing to report.—	Regt
	3/6/18		Nothing to report.—	Regt
	4/6/18		Nothing to report.—	Regt
	5/6/18		Nothing to report.—	Regt
	6/6/18		Nothing to report.—	Regt
	7/6/18		Nothing to report.—	Regt
	8/6/18		Nothing to report.—	Regt
	9/6/18		Nothing to report.—	Regt
	10/6/18		Nothing to report.—	Regt
	11/6/18		Nothing to report.—	Regt
	12/6/18		Nothing to report.—	Regt
	13/6/18		Nothing to report.—	Regt
	14/6/18		Nothing to report.—	Regt
	15/6/18		Nothing to report.—	Regt
	16/6/18		Nothing to report:—	Regt

Army Form C. 2118.

WAR DIARY

INTELLIGENCE SUMMARY

2/3RD WEST RIDING FIELD AMBULANCE
JUNE 1918.   SHEET 4

ORIGINAL

Place	Date	Hour	Summary of Events and Information	Remarks and references to Appendices
P.A.S.	17/6/18		nothing to report.	
	18/6/18		nothing to report.	
	19/6/18		nothing to report.	
	20/6/18		nothing to report.	
	21/6/18		nothing to report.	
	22/6/18		nothing to report.	
	23/6/18		Six cases of Pyrexia were admitted to Hospital today suffering from the usual P.B.O. in the following respects - Sudden onset (about 12 hours) coryza, some bronchitis, pain behind the eyes, and absence of skin pains. They were diagnosed as INFLUENZA.	
	24/6/18		O.C. 50th Field Ambulance visited the unit with a view to taking over. CAPTAIN FREW and 59 O.R. RAMC reported from duty with 2/2 W.R.F.Amb. Thirteen Cases of Influenza were admitted to Hospital.	
	25/6/18.		CAPTAIN MACMILLAN and one tuberculosis with 1 E.S wagon (workcart) proceeded to report to O.C. 1/3 East Lancs Field Ambulance at MONT RENAULT FARM for duty at the Corps Rest Station.	

Army Form C. 2118.

WAR DIARY

~~INTELLIGENCE SUMMARY.~~

(Erase heading not required.)

2/3RD WEST RIDING FIELD AMBULANCE
/ JUNE 1918 SHEET 1
ORIGINAL

Instructions regarding War Diaries and Intelligence Summaries are contained in F. S. Regs., Part II. and the Staff Manual respectively. Title pages will be prepared in manuscript.

Place	Date	Hour	Summary of Events and Information	Remarks and references to Appendices
P.A.S.	25/6/18	2 pm	The unit moved to billets at TERRAMESNIL, the R.A.M.C. personnel and MOTOR WAGGONS WORTH being bussed to BRUILLE and completing the journey on foot, the remainder of the unit and transport proceeding via FAMECHON, THIEVRES, SARTON	RgW
		6 p.m.	The 27 bearers who were attached to the R.M.O.s of the 187 Inf. Brigade rejoined the unit	RgW
TERRASMESNIL	26/6/18		nothing to report:-	RgW
	27/6/18		nothing to report.	RgW
	28/6/18		nothing to report.	RgW
	29/6/18		nothing to report.	RgW
	30/6/18		A table shewing the rates of admission of P.U.O and influenza from the 23. to the 30. is attached.	RgW

RgWilliamson
LIEUT. COLONEL R.A.M.C.
COMMDG. 2/3rd. WEST RIDING FIELD AMBULANCE

2/3RD
WEST RIDING
FIELD AMBULANCE

Admissions for P. U. O. and influenza.

APPENDIX I

INFLUENZA — RED.   P.U.O — BLACK.

June..	23.	24.	25.	26.	27.	28.	29.	30.

2/3RD WEST RIDING FIELD AMBULANCE.

No............
Date............

LIEUT. COLONEL R.A.M.C.
COMMDG. 2/3rd. WEST RIDING FIELD AMBULANCE

MEDICAL

CONFIDENTIAL   ORIGINAL

July 1918   Vol 19

2/3 WEST RIDING FIELD AMBULANCE   14/3/31

WAR DIARY
OF
2/3 WEST RIDING FIELD AMBULANCE

July 1918

VOLUME XIX

COMMITTEE FOR THE
MEDICAL HISTORY OF THE WAR
Date 6 SEP. 1918

MEDICAL
Army Form C. 2118.

WAR DIARY
INTELLIGENCE SUMMARY
(Erase heading not required.)

2/3rd West Riding Field Ambulance
July 1918
PAGE 1

Place	Date	Hour	Summary of Events and Information	Remarks and references to Appendices
TERRAMESNIL	1/7/18		Nothing to report	REW
	2/7/18		Nothing to report	REW
	3		Nothing to report	REW
	4		Nothing to report	REW
	5		Nothing to report	REW
	6		A.D.M.S. 62nd Division inspected the Unit	REW
	7		Nothing to report	REW
	8		Nothing to report	REW
	9		Nothing to report	REW
	10		Nothing to report	REW
	11		Nothing to report	REW
	12		Nothing to report	REW
	13		Received warning order. Unit moves - programme showing routes & area of Manin I Sous	REW
	14		Capts Sheppard & Orwin proceeded on billeting party to new area	REW
	15		Unit marched to DOULLENS to entrain	REW

WAR DIARY
INTELLIGENCE SUMMARY

Army Form C. 2118.

1/3 West Riding Field Ambulance
July 1918
PAGE 2

Place	Date	Hour	Summary of Events and Information	Remarks and references to Appendices
MAILLY	26/19/18		Unit detrained & billeted in Field Camp.	
GRAND				
EGYPT	1-17/7/18		Unit marched to Elbury and Cape & Mevany 1 pm	Ops
LIMOGES				
	18/1/18		CAPT IRWIN with Bearer Division & Section equipment proceeded	
			to TOURS on MARNE - CAPT MA MILNER with rest & bearer	
			on rest to VERTUS & taken to hospital private	Ops
			Remainder of unit & transport moved to VERTUS	Ops
VERTUS	19/7/18		CAPT IRWIN's party moved to ST IMOGES & Divisional sent forward	
			to 2/1 W R F Amb. 3 huts were taken over from the French au	
			VERTUS & one left in charge of packing on the Bulk supplied	
			At 6 pm relieved to move to SEZANNE to open a CCS.	Ops
			unit left VERTUS arrived at SEZANNE 11.30 am & found Tent Section	
SEZANNE	20/7/18		already arrived. Returned to CHAMPILLON to empty M A C vans	Ops
CHAMPILLON	21/7/18		Transport moved from VERTUS to CHAMPILLON. 24 Bearers seat to M D S & M A C	Ops
			NIGHT NORTH went to SERIMES & PIERRE NORTREW	Ops

T2134. Wt. W708—776. 500000. 4/15. Sir J. C. & S.

Army Form C. 2118.

WAR DIARY
INTELLIGENCE SUMMARY.
(Erase heading not required.)

2/3 West Riding Field Ambulance
ORIGINAL. July 1918. Page 3.

Instructions regarding War Diaries and Intelligence Summaries are contained in F. S. Regs., Part II. and the Staff Manual respectively. Title pages will be prepared in manuscript.

Place	Date	Hour	Summary of Events and Information	Remarks and references to Appendices
CHAMPILLON	22/7/18		Nothing to report.	
	23/7/18		Nothing to report	
	24/7/18		Visited the forward area. 1/2 TR & W.R. Coy buried according to B.S.	See Appendix II
SERMIER	28/7/18		H Qs moved to SERMIER. Took over A.D.S from 2/1 W.R.E Amb.	
			Took charge of evacuation from forward area which was being carried out by the officer 1/c Rear Group — 2/2 W.R Amb at Chigwar from line.	
			Line of evacuation established in and at NANTEUIL, bringing motor hut.	
	29/7/18		51st Division. Brit'sh sent in during the evening.	
			Visited NANTEUIL, ST DENIS & 2/4 3rd in good order. 1 O.M.S. & 2 Offr	
	2/7/18		Nothing to report.	
POURCY	28/7/18		A.D.S. moved to POURCY. a new line of evacuation via hu[?]	See Appendix III
	29/7/18		2 Mos + 17 O.R. sent to walking wounded post B.S.W. NANT[EUIL]	See Appendix IV
	30/7/18		Nine stretcher bearers and relieved as transport beasts. 3 injured 8	
ST IMOGES	31/7/18		Another 2 Mos + party from NANTEUIL report and unit.	
				P. Williams
				Lieut Colonel R.A.M.C.
				COMMDG. 2/3rd WEST RIDING FIELD AMBULANCE

2/3rd West Riding
Field Ambulance.

APPENDIX. 1.

Programme of Training.

	9.a.m.	9.45.	10.45.	2.p.m.
Wednesday 26/6/18	Fatigues	Cleaning of Equipment	-	C.O's Inspection.
Thursday 27/6/18	Physical Drill	Route March	Route March	Kit Inspection
Friday 28/6/18	Physical Drill	Squad Drill	Saluting Drill	Insp. Gas Appliances.
Saturday 29/6/18	Physical Drill	Commanding Officers Inspection (& Transport)		
Sunday 30/6/18	Bathing Parades	Medical Inspection and	Church Parades	
Monday 1/7/18	Physical Drill	Stretcher Drill	Loading drill in S.B.R.	Lecture. Application of Thomas Splint.
Tuesday 2/7/18	Physical Drill	Route March	Route March	Lecture: Arrest of haemorrhage.
Wednesday 3/7/18	Physical Drill	Squad Drill	Saluting Drill	- - - - -
Thursday 4/7/18	Physical Drill	Route March	Route March	Pay Parade
Friday 5/7/18	Physical Drill	Stretcher Drill	Wagon Drill	Application of Thomas Splint.
Saturday 6/7/18	Commanding Officer's Inspection including transport			- - - - -
Sunday 7/7/18	Bathing Parades	Medical Inspection	Church Parades	- - - - -
Monday 8/7/18	Physical Drill	Route March	Route March	Inspection Gas Appliances and Gas Drill.
Tuesday 9/7/18	Physical Drill	Stretcher Drill	Wagon Drill	- - - - -
Wednesday 10/7/18	Physical Drill	Route March	Route March	- - - - -
Thursday 11/7/18	Physical Drill	Squad Drill	Saluting Drill	Kit Inspection
Friday 12/7/18	Physical drill	Route March	Route March	- - - - -

Appendix 2.   Evacuation from 185th Infantry Brigade.

Map Reference
SOISSONS Sheet 22.
1/100,000.

TWO Regimental Aid Posts at approximately 4.K.99.26, which evacuate through Relay Posts to ECEUIL FARM.
TWO Regimental Aid Posts at 5.K.99.91 (Pourcy) and ONE R.A.P. at 5.L.04.87 - (which is a combined Relay and Regimental Aid Post). These evacuate to a quarry on the POURCY-SERMIERS ROAD where a Daimler Car stands, and from there to the Advanced Dressing Station, SERMIERS.
One Regimental Aid Post at 4.L.38.01 evacuates to Eceuil Farm.

                                            P.G.Williamson
                                    Lieutenant Colonel, R.A.M.C.T.
                        Commanding 2/3rd West Riding Field Ambulance.

Appendix 3.

Map reference
SOISSONS Sheet 22.
1/100,000.

Arrangements for evacuation from the LEFT SECTOR in conjunction with the 51st Division.

From Regimental Aid Posts to First Relay Post at northern edge of BOIS de COURTON, ¼" S.E. of the N in BULLIN, and then by hand carriage to Car Loading Post, St. DENIS, and thence to Main Dressing Station by Motor Ambulances.

<u>Walking Wounded.</u>   to post in edge of wood, ¼" N. of the V in CORMOVEUX then by Horse Ambulance to Main Dressing Station.

<u>Disposition of Personnel.</u>

<u>First Relay Post.</u>   One Medical Officer and Nine squads.
<u>Car Loading Post.</u>   One N.C.O. and 2 squads.

P.G.Williamson
Lieutenant Colonel, R.A.M.C.T.
Commanding 2/3 West Riding Field Ambulance.

Appendix 4. continued.

MARFAUX Collecting Post and conveyed to NANTEUIL.

Advanced Dressing Station at FOURCY for Walking Wounded and Stretcher cases. Evacuation to NANTEUIL by Motor and Horse Ambulances.
Walking Wounded evacuated from NANTEUIL by Motor Lorries.
Car Control Post at St. DENIS.

R.␣Williamson
Lieutenant Colonel, R.A.M.C.T.
Commanding 2/3 West Riding Field Ambulance.

Appendix 4.

Map reference.
SOISSONS SHEET 22   Line of Evacuation 28th July, 1918.
1/100,000.

Regimental Aid Posts.

2/4th K. O. Y. L. I.)	200 yards along road leading
2/4th York and Lancs.)	N.E. from MAPPES.
5th K. O. Y. L. I. —	Quarry 700 yards along road leading N.E. from MAPPES.
5th Devons.)	
8th West Yorks.)	in CHAUMUZY
2/5th West Yorks.)	
2/4th Hants.)	
2/4th West Ridings)	in Marfaux.
2/5th West Ridings —	ESPILLY.
9th Durham L. I. —	CUITRON.

Motor ambulances proceed as far as CHAUMUZY, cases are also collected at

MEDICAL

CONFIDENTIAL

ORIGINAL

August 1918
MO/3200

WAR DIARY

OF

2/3 West Riding Field Amb.

August 1918 — Vol. XX

COMMITTEE FOR THE
MEDICAL HISTORY OF THE WAR
Date 5 OCT 1918

Army Form C. 2118.

WAR DIARY
INTELLIGENCE SUMMARY
(Erase heading not required.)

ORIGINAL

2/3 West Riding
Field Ambulance
Sheet No 1   August 1918

Place	Date	Hour	Summary of Events and Information	Remarks and references to Appendices
ST. IMOGES	1/8/18		The unit proceeded with 185th Brigade via EPERNAY and CHOUILLY to billets at the CITE AUBAN MOUET.	RgW
CITE AUBAN MOUET	2/8/18		nothing to report.	RgW
	3/8/18		nothing to report.	RgW
	4/8/18		Marched to VERTUS where the unit was entrained. The motor transport went on to FERE CHAMPENOISE and entrained with the M.T. Coy.	RgW
	5/8/18		Detrained at Candas and marched to Mont RENAULT FARM. Took over the Rest Station from 1/48 Field Ambulance 63 (RN) Division.	RgW
MONT RENAULT FM	6/8/18		Took over the Rest Station from 1/48 Field Ambulance 63.(RN) Division: The Corps Rest Station has accommodation for 250 patients in huts and the patients are classified under three headings. Medical Surgical and Convalescent. There is a large dining hall, a bathhouse with a Jacob's chamber, and the naval officers - packstore, dispensary, storeset. A motor lorry for the conveyance of rations from AUXI LE CHATEAU, a motor water tank, and a FODEN disinfector are attached.	RgW
	7/8/18			RgW
"	8/8/18		nothing to report.	RgW

Army Form C. 2118.

WAR DIARY
INTELLIGENCE SUMMARY

2/3 West Riding Field Ambulance

(Erase heading not required.)

ORIGINAL

August 1918
Sheet No 2

Place	Date	Hour	Summary of Events and Information	Remarks and references to Appendices
MONT RENAULT FARM	9/8/18		nothing to report.	RJW
"	10/8/18		nothing to report.	RJW
"	11/8/18		nothing to report.	RJW
"	12/8/18		nothing to report.	RJW
"	13/8/18		nothing to report.	RJW
"	14/8/18		nothing to report.	RJW
"	15/8/18		nothing to report.	RJW
"	16/8/18		nothing to report.	RJW
"	17/8/18		nothing to report.	RJW
"	18/8/18		Preparations were made to transfer the Corps Rest Station to the CITROEN DOULLENS.	RJW
"	19/8/18		Two officers and 1 tent subdivision of the 1/3 EAST LANCS F.A. arrived to take over the Rest Station.	RJW
"	20/8/18	5 a.m.	The unit left MONT RENAULT FARM marching via LE MEILLARD, MESEROLLES, BARLY, BOUQUEMAISON, IVERGNY.	RJW
		12.30 pm	Arrived SUC ST LEGER – and reported to 187 Inf Brigade for orders.	RJW
		9.45 pm	Marched under the orders of 187 Inf Brigade via SOMBRIN to SAULTY.	RJW

Army Form C. 2118.

WAR DIARY
INTELLIGENCE SUMMARY
(Erase heading not required.)

ORIGINAL

1/3 West Riding Field Ambulance
Sheet No 3   August 1918

Place	Date	Hour	Summary of Events and Information	Remarks and references to Appendices
SAULTY	21/8/18	10.30 p.m.	Marched via MONDICOURT, POMMERA.	RgW
	22/8/18	3.0 a.m	Arrived DOULLENS.	RgW
		9 a.m	Advanced party left for MONT RENAULT FARM to take over the Corps Rest Station	RgW
		10 a.m	Remainder of Personnel and transport left for MONT RENAULT FARM via OCCOCHES MESEROLLES and LE MEILLARD.	RgW
		2 p.m	Arrived MONT RENAULT FARM.	RgW
MONT RENAULT FARM	23/8/18	9 am	Unit moved to DOULLENS after handing over C.R.S to 111 F. Amb	RgW
DOULLENS	24/8/18	2 am	Arrived DOULLENS	RgW
		8 am	Transport moved to BIENVILLERS. MAJOR WIGGLESWORTH + personnel moved by lorry to MONCHY au BOIS. Two squads + driver sent to each battalion of 187 Iny Bde.	RgW
BIENVILLERS	25/8/18		Two MOs + Lieut Williamson sent for duty to No 3 Canadian C.C.S. Ambulances sent to report to 2/1 W.Riding F Amb.	RgW
	26/8/18		MAJOR SNEDDON + Lieut Williamson sent for duty to 2/2 W Riding F Amb	RgW
	27/8/18		Nothing to report	RgW

WAR DIARY

INTELLIGENCE SUMMARY

Army Form C. 2118.

1/3 West Riding Field Ambulance

Sheet No 4 August 1918

Place	Date	Hour	Summary of Events and Information	Remarks and references to Appendices
BIENVILLERS	28.8.18		Transport & HQ sig unit moved to AYETTE	RgW
AYETTE	29.8.18		The MO's + bd' adversion returned to unit from C.C.S.	RgW
"	30-8-18		Nothing to report	RgW
"	31-8-18		Nothing to report	RgW

R.G. Williamson
LIEUT. COLONEL R.A.M.O.
1/3rd WEST RIDING FIELD AMBULANCE

MEDICAL

ORIGINAL

CONFIDENTIAL

WAR DIARY
OF
2/3rd WEST RIDING FIELD AMBULANCE
SEPTEMBER 1918

VOLUME XXI

Army Form C. 2118.

WAR DIARY
or
INTELLIGENCE SUMMARY.
(Erase heading not required.)

2/3 WEST RIDING FIELD AMBULANCE
SHEET No. 1
ORIGINAL SEPTEMBER 1918

Instructions regarding War Diaries and Intelligence Summaries are contained in F.S. Regs., Part II. and the Staff Manual respectively. Title pages will be prepared in manuscript.

Place	Date	Hour	Summary of Events and Information	Remarks and references to Appendices
AMETTE	1/9/18		Nothing to report.	RFW
COURCELLES	2/9/18		The unit moved to COURCELLES occupying tents and bivouacs.	RFW
"	3/9/18		The bearers returned from 2/1st West R.F.A. and Battalions, the tent subdivision from the 2/2 W.R.F.A.	RFW
"	4/9/18		Nothing to report.	RFW
"	5/9/18		Nothing to report.	RFW
"	6/9/18		Nothing to report.	RFW
"	7/9/18		Nothing to report.	RFW
"	8/9/18		Nothing to report.	RFW
"	9/9/18		Nothing to report.	RFW
BEHAGNIES	10/9/18		The unit moved from COURCELLES to BEHAGNIES. Visited the forward area with the DADMS. The unit marched behind 187 Brigade to billets in VERU WOOD. T 31. d. 3 & 4 (57 c). A bearer division under Captain PICKLES reported from 2/1 W.R.F. Ambulance. Two bearer squads with one nurse were attached to each R.M.O. of 187 Brigade.	RFW
"	11/9/18		Major WIGGLESWORTH, Captain FREW with two NCOs and bearers proceeded to	RFW

MEDICAL

Army Form C. 2118.

2/5 WEST RIDING
FIELD AMBULANCE
SEPTEMBER 1918

SHEET N° 2.

WAR DIARY
of
INTELLIGENCE SUMMARY.
(Erase heading not required.)

ORIGINAL

Instructions regarding War Diaries and Intelligence Summaries are contained in F. S. Regs., Part II. and the Staff Manual respectively. Title pages will be prepared in manuscript.

Place	Date	Hour	Summary of Events and Information	Remarks and references to Appendices
			established the bearer posts on the lines of evacuation. The headquarters of the unit were moved to ROYAKCOURT when an advanced dressing station was established at P.10.c.4.4. (57c)	RLW
			A walking wounded and car control post was established at P.7.b.0.5 (BERTINCOURT)	RLW
			One tent subdivision was sent to the 2/2 W.R.F.A. for work at the Main Dressing Station.	RLW
			20 men were received from each Infantry Brigade and 50 from the Reinforcement Camp to supplement the bearers.	RLW
ROYAKCOURT	12/9/18.		Lines of evacuation had been established as given in Appendix I.	
			A further reinforcement of 2 NCOs and 26 men were received from 2/1 and 2/2 West Riding Field Ambulance.	
			By 8 P.M. a total of 162 stretcher cases had passed through the Advanced Dressing Station.	RLW
"	13/9/18		Visited the bearer posts. The line of evacuation was modified as shown in Appendix II.	RLW

Army Form C. 2118.

WAR DIARY
INTELLIGENCE SUMMARY.
(Erase heading not required.)

2/3 WEST RIDING FIELD AMBULANCE
SEPTEMBER 1918.

ORIGINAL

Sheet No 3

Place	Date	Hour	Summary of Events and Information	Remarks and references to Appendices
ROYAUCOURT	14/9/18		The transport lines were moved from J.31.d.3.4. to evacuation normal.	
"	15/9/18		G.O.C. 62 Division visited the A.D.S.	Sgd
"	16/9/18		The forward Area was handed over to the 142 Division, and the A.D.S. at ROYAUCOURT to the 7th FIELD AMBULANCE.	Sgd
"			The unit proceeded to BILLETS at BEHAGNIES.	Sgd
BEHAGNIES	17/9/18		The bearers were returned to their respective units.	Sgd
"	18/9/18		nothing to report.	Sgd
"	19/9/18		nothing to report.	Sgd
"	20/9/18		nothing to report.	Sgd
"	21/9/18		nothing to report.	Sgd
"	22/9/18		nothing to report.	Sgd
"	23/9/18		nothing to report.	Sgd
"	24/9/18		nothing to report.	Sgd
"	25/9/18		1 Officer, 2 NCO's and 8 Squads of bearers from the 2/1st W.R. Field Ambulance reported for duty. Two Squads and one runner were sent to each battalion of 187 I.B.	Sgd

Army Form C. 2118.

2/3 WEST RIDING
FIELD AMBULANCE SHEET
SEPTEMBER 1918 No 4

ORIGINAL

WAR DIARY
or
INTELLIGENCE SUMMARY.
(Erase heading not required.)

Place	Date	Hour	Summary of Events and Information	Remarks and references to Appendices
BEAUMETZ	25/9/18		The unit proceeded via BAPAUME and BANCOURT to a site at O.S.d. 9.9 (57c)	egw
BERTINCOURT	26/9/18		Two squads and one Daimler car were posted at J.35.d.8.9 to collect casualties from the Brigade waiting to move into their battle positions. 80 Stretcher bearers were received from the Infantry Brigades. All available cars and horse ambulances were received from 2/1st and 2/2 W.R.F. Ambulances.	egw
"	27/9/18		The headquarters of the unit were moved to K.32.b.6.7 where the ADS was taken over from 142 F. Ambulance. A collecting post for Daimler's lorry established at P.18.a.9.6. The wounded became evacuated from the ADS via HERMIES to the MDS at RUYAUCOURT. MAJOR WIGGLESWORTH, CAPTAIN FREW, CAPTAIN PRINGLE who had gone forward established relay and car post in accordance with the attached appendix III. A walking wounded post was also established at J.35.d.9.9 from which walking wounded were conveyed by Horse Ambulances to the M.D.S.	egw

Army Form C. 2118.

WAR DIARY

INTELLIGENCE SUMMARY

(Erase heading not required.)

2/3 WEST RIDING FIELD AMBULANCE SHEET No.5
SEPTEMBER 1918

ORIGINAL

Place	Date	Hour	Summary of Events and Information	Remarks and references to Appendices
YORKSHIRE BANK.	28/9/18		Evacuation as shown in Appendix III	RgW
	29/9/18		Forward A.D.S. established at RIBECOURT.	RgW
	30/9/18		Headquarters moved to The A.D.S. at RIBECOURT. Posts at P18 a 9.6 and T.35.d.9.9. were abolished. Walking wounded posts were established at HAVRINCOURT, YORKSHIRE BANK, and CLAYTON CROSS.	RgW

R.W.Hampton
LIEUT COLONEL

Commanding 2/3 West Riding Field Ambulance.

APPENDIX I
AND
APPENDIX II

APPENDIX 1.   Map reference Sheet 57 C.

Line of Evacuation

First Phase.

REGIMENTAL AID POSTS

K.32.d.0.5.	Q.2.a.6.9.	Q.3.a.4.4.	Q.2.c.2.2.
2/4 Y & L.	2/4 KOYLI	2/4 W.Ridings	2/4 Hants
5th KOYLI		5 W.Ridings	

1st RELAY POST
J.35.d.9.6

1st RELAY POST
Q.8.a.1.9

2nd RELAY POST
J.36 cent.

2nd RELAY POST
P.12.b.6.6

3rd RELAY POST
J.35.d.6.9

CAR LOADING POST
P.5.c.1.9.
By Field Ambulance
Cars
to

CAR LOADING POST
P.11.b.6.3
By Field Ambulance
Cars
to

ADVANCED DRESSING STATION.
P.10.c.4.4.

and on in
Field Ambulance cars
to

MAIN DRESSING STATION.
O.4.d.9.9.
(2/2 W. R. Field Ambulance)

Walking Wounded

Walking Wounded Collecting Posts.

P.17.d.5.6.   P.10.a.9.6.

By Horse Ambulances
to

Ambulance Control Post.
P.7.b.0.5

and on in
Horse Ambulances to

MAIN DRESSING STATION.
O.4.d.9.9.
(2/2 W. R. Field Ambulance)

R G Williamson
LIEUT COLONEL
Commanding 2/3 West Riding Field Ambulance.

APPENDIX 2.

Map Reference
Sheet 57 C.

Line of Evacuation.

Second Phase.

REGIMENTAL AID POSTS.

K.32.b.2.7.	K.32.b.4.7.	K.32.d.0.5.	K.26.d.6.9.	K.33.b.3.0.	Q.8.a.2.4.	Q.2.c.2.2.	Q.2.a.6.9.	Q.3.a.4.4.
5th Devons	5th D. L. I	2/4 Y & L	5th KOYLI	2/20 Londons	8 W.Yorks	2/4 Hants	2/4 KOYLI	2/4 W.Ridings 5 W.Ridings

FORD CAR LOADING POST.
K.32.b.3.3.

RELAY POST.
K.31.a.2.2
By Trolley
to

DAIMLER LOADING POST.
J.35.d.5.9.
By Field Ambulance
Cars
to

DAIMLER LOADING POST.
Q.8.a.1.9.
By Field Ambulance
Cars
to

ADVANCED DRESSING STATION.
P.10.c.4.4.
and on in
Field Ambulance Cars
to
MAIN DRESSING STATION.
O.4.d.9.9.
(2/2 W. R. Field Ambulance)

RELAY POST.
Q.2.d.9.0

Reg Manson
Lieutenant Colonel, R.A.M.C.T.
Commanding 2/3 West Riding Field Ambulance.

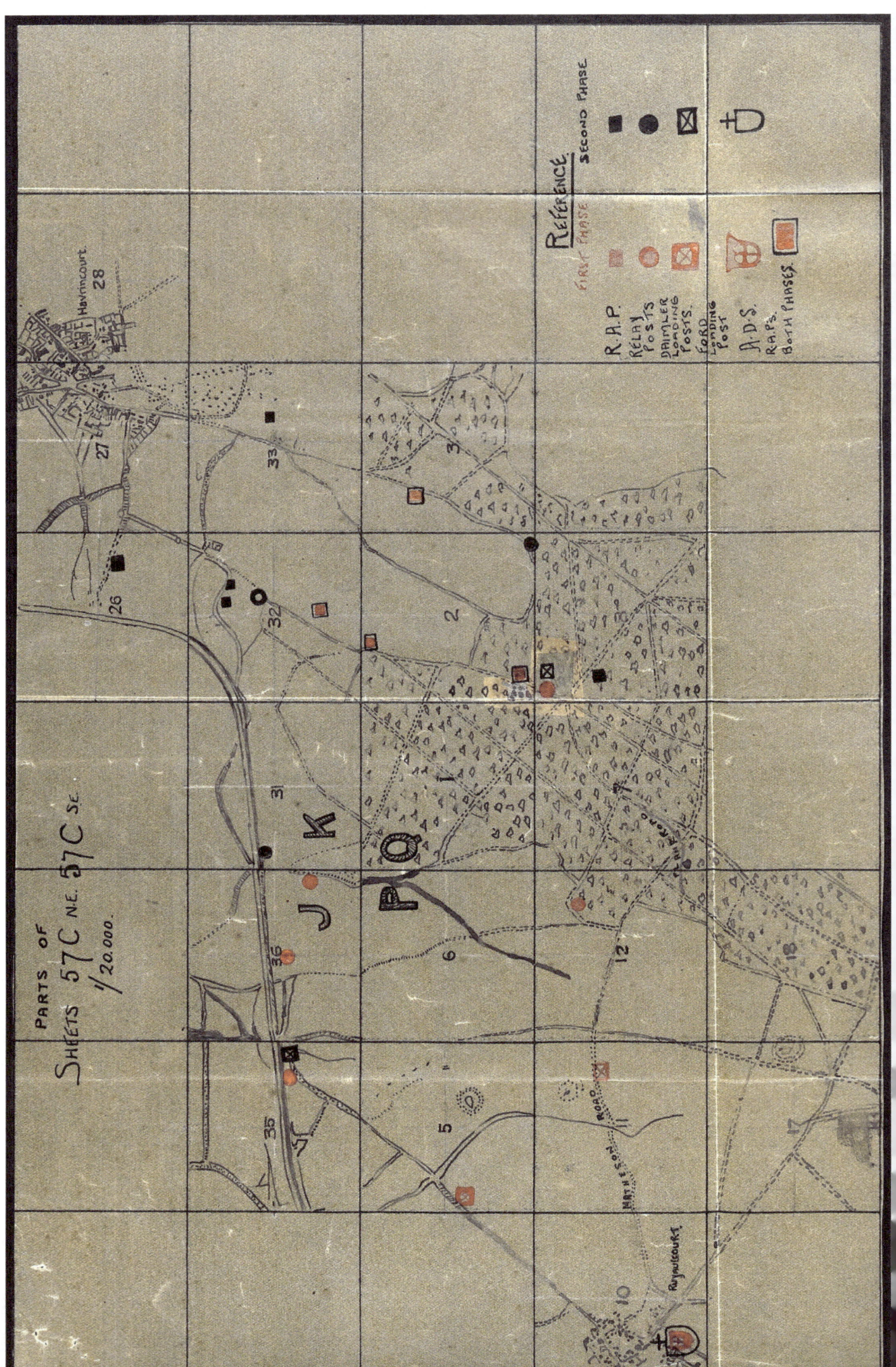

APPENDIX III

2/3RD
WEST RIDING
FIELD AMBULANCE.
Sept
30/18

APPENDIX III.   Map Reference Sheets 57 C & 27 B.

OPERATIONS 27th September, 1918 to 30th September, 1918.

Lines of Evacuation.

Regimental Aid Posts.   12 Noon 27/9/18.

2/4 York and Lancs	K.29.c.5.9	Evacuation from R.A.P's by hand
5 K.O.Y.L.I.	K.29.c.5.9	carriage to Ford Car Post at K.34.a.
2/4 K.O.Y.L.I.	K.28.d.5.3	7.7. By Ford Car to A.D.S at K.32
2/20 LONDON REGT.	L.19.c.7.3	b.4.7. and on by Daimler Car to M.D.S
5 DEVON REGIMENT	L.19.a.4.4	RUYAULCOURT. Walking Wounded by
8 WEST YORKS.	L.20.b.8.6	Horse Ambulances from W.W.C.P. at
		J.35.d.9.9. to M.D.S. RUYAULCOURT.

Regimental Aid Posts.   10.a.m. 28/9/1918.

2/4 York & Lancs	K.30.b.9.5.	Evacuation from R.A.P's to Ford
5 K.O.Y.L.I	K.30.b.8.5	Car Post at K.34.a.7.7. Later,
2/4 K.O.Y.L.I	K.28.d.5.3	Ford Cars were run up the
2/20 LONDON REGT.	L.20.c.9.9	FLESQUIERES-RIBECOURT ROAD and
5 DEVON REGIMENT	L.19.b.2.1	Daimler Car Post established at
8 WEST YORKS.	L.20.a.4.7	K.24.a.3.8. Ford Cars were pushed
2/4 WEST RIDING RGT	L.20.a.9.5	forward later as the R.A.P's
5 WEST RIDING RGT	L.19.c.3.7	advanced, cases being evacuated by
2/4 HANTS. REGIMENT	L.19.b.1.8	Ford Car from L.20.d.6.4. to
		K.24.a.3.8. and thence by Daimler
		Car to the A.D.S. at K.32.b.4.7.
		and on my Daimler Car to M.D.S.

Regimental Aid Posts.   29/9/1918.

2/4 York and Lancs	L.29.b.2.1)	Evacuations through Relay Posts at and L.21.b.9.1
5 K.O.Y.L.I.	L.29.b.2.1)..	L.28.b.cent. to Ford Car Post L.25.a.
2/4 K.O.Y.L.I.	L.29.b.2.1)	8.8. To Daimler Post K.24.a.3.6 & MDS
2/20 LONDON REGT.	L.20.c.9.9)	Evacuations via Ford Car Post at
5 DEVON REGIMENT	L.19.b.2.1)	L.20.d.6.4. and Daimler Post at
8 WEST YORKS.	L.20.a.4.7)..	K.24.a.3.8. to A.D.S. RIBECOURT,
2/4 West Riding Rgt	L.20.a.9.5)	L.25.b.2.6. and on in Daimler
5 West Riding Regt	L.19.c.3.7)	Cars to Main Dressing Station,
2/4 Hants. Regt.	L.19.b.1.8.)	RUYAULCOURT.

Regimental Aid Posts.   30/9/1918.

2/4 York and Lancs	L.28.b.3.2	Evacuation through Relay Posts at
5 K.O.Y.L.I	L.29.b.2.1	L.24.c.6.4 and L.23.c.1.1 to Ford
2/4 K.O.Y.L.I	L.29.a.7.3	Car Post at L.22.a.9.3. Thence by
2/20 LONDON REGT.	L.24.c.6.4	Ford Car to A.D.S. RIBECOURT,
5 DEVON REGIMENT	G.20.d.7.2	L.25.b.2.6 and on in Daimler Cars
8 WEST YORKS.	G.27.central	to M.D.S.
2/4 WEST RIDING Rgt	L.21.b.3.6	Walking Wounded from A.D.S. RIBECOURT
5 WEST RIDING Rgt	L.22.a.7.6	in Horse Ambulances to The Square,
2/4 HANTS. REGT.	L.21.c.6.7	Havrincourt Village. Then directed
		down the road to YORKSHIRE BANK -
		K.32.b.4.7. - and on plank road to
		CLAYTON CROSS. Then by Horse
		Ambulances to Main Dressing Station
		RUYAULCOURT.

2/3RD WEST RIDING FIELD AMBULANCE.
No.............
Date............

30th September, 1918.

B.G. Williamson
Lieutenant Colonel, R.A.M.C.T.
Commanding 2/3rd West Riding Field Ambulance.

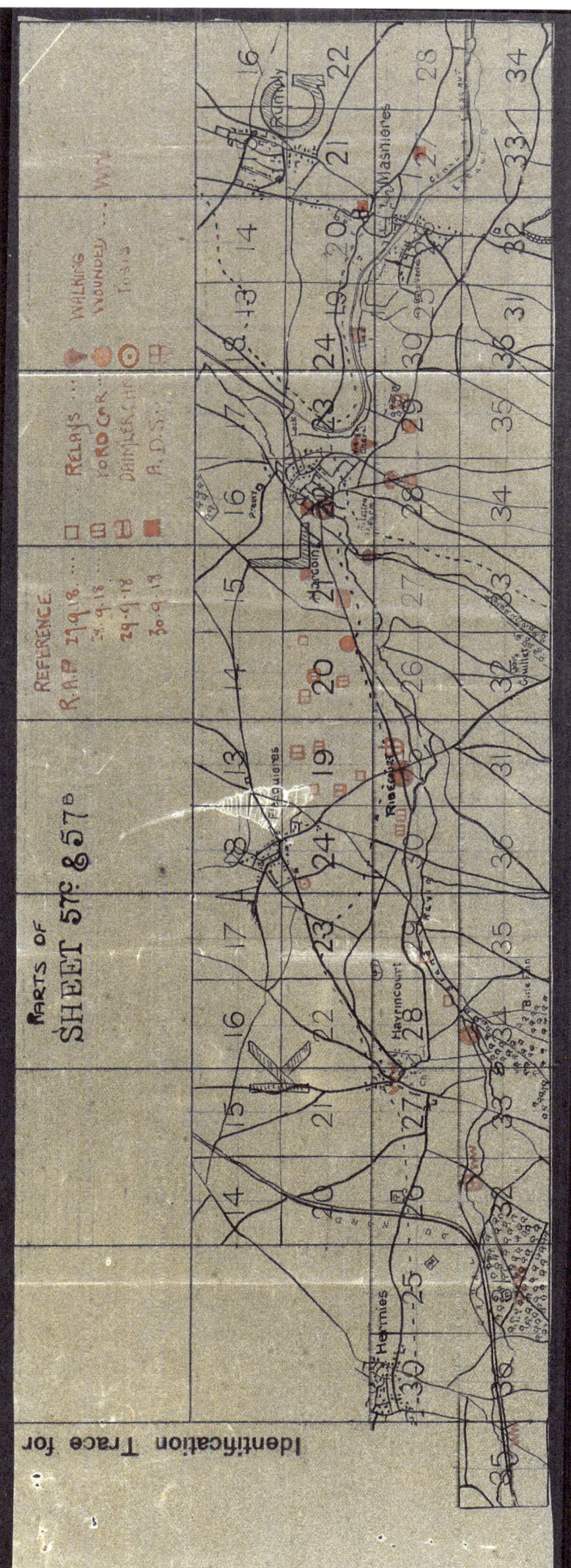

MEDICAL
ORIGINAL

CONFIDENTIAL

WAR DIARY
OF
2/3 WEST RIDING FIELD AMBULANCE

OCTOBER 1918

VOLUME XXII

WAR DIARY

Army Form C. 2118.

MEDICAL

2/3 WEST RIDING FIELD AMBULANCE OCTOBER 1918 SHEET 1

ORIGINAL

INTELLIGENCE SUMMARY
(Erase heading not required.)

Place	Date	Hour	Summary of Events and Information	Remarks and references to Appendices
RIBECOURT	1/10/18		The ADS and posts in the forward area were handed over to 8th Field Ambulance. The headquarters of the unit moved to YORKSHIRE BANK. The bearer division of 2/1st W.R.F Ambulance remained attached to this unit.	
YORKSHIRE BANK	2/10/18		Nothing to report.	
"	3/10/18		Nothing to report.	
"	4/10/18		Nothing to report.	
"	5/10/18		Nothing to report.	
"	6/10/18		Nothing to report.	
"	7/10/18		Nothing to report.	
"	8/10/18		8 bearers and 1 runner were sent to each battalion of 167 Inf. Brigade. The unit moved from transport lines at RUYAUCOURT and beth at YORKSHIRE BANK to old ADS site at RIBECOURT. The remainder of the bearer division of 2/1" were attached to 2/2 W.R.F Ambulance.	
"	9/10/18			
RIBECOURT	10/10/18		The unit moved from RIBECOURT to billets in RUMILLY.	
RUMILLY	11/10/18		The unit moved with 167 Inf. Brigade to billets at BOISTRANCOURT. I. a. 99. 57 B.	

WAR DIARY

Army Form C. 2118.

2/3 WEST RIDING FIELD AMBULANCE
OCTOBER 1918
SHEET 11

ORIGINAL

Place	Date	Hour	Summary of Events and Information	Remarks and references to Appendices
BOISTRANCOURT	12/10/18		Nothing to report.	RgW
"	13/10/18		The unit proceeded with 187 Inf. Brigade via ESTOURMEL to billets at CATTENIERES	RgW
CATTENIERES	14/10/18		Nothing to report.	RgW
"	15/10/18		Nothing to report.	RgW
"	16/10/18		Nothing to report	RgW
"	17/10/18		CAPTAIN J.M. PRINGLE with one tent subdivision took over the D.R.S. at CARNIERES from 2/2 WEST RIDING F. Ambu. Two clerks were sent to the MDS. GUARDS Division to relieve 62 Division Casualties.	RgW
"	18/10/18		Nothing to report.	RgW
"	19/10/18		Moved from CATTENIERES to BEVILLERS. One tent subdivision was sent for duty to the MDS. Guards Div. Three horse ambulances and two Ford cars were sent to the 2/2 W.R.F Ambulance	RgW
BEVILLERS	20/10/18		Nothing to report.	RgW
"	21/10/18		Nothing to report.	RgW

WAR DIARY

Army Form C. 2118.

2/3 WEST RIDING FIELD AMBULANCE

OCTOBER 1918 SHEET II

ORIGINAL

Place	Date	Hour	Summary of Events and Information	Remarks and references to Appendices
	22/10/18		nothing to report	
	23/10/18		The unit moved to CARNIERES to form a Corps Rest Station in site of GUARDS M.D.S.	
CARNIERES	24/10/18		D.D.M.S. VI Corps visited the C.R.S.	W.S.
"	25/10/18		nothing to report	W.S.
	26/10/18		nothing to report	W.S.
	27/10/18		D.D.M.S. VI Corps and G.O.C. 62 Division visited the Corps Rest Station	W.S.
	28/10/18		nothing to report	W.S.
	29/10/18		nothing to report	W.S.
	30/10/18		nothing to report	W.S.
	31/10/18		nothing to report	W.S.

W. Saunders Major

MEDICAL

CONFIDENTIAL

WAR - DIARY

OF

2/3 WEST RIDING FIELD AMBULANCE

FROM NOVEMBER 1ST 1918 TO NOVEMBER 30TH 1918

VOLUME XXII

MEDICAL

Army Form C. 2118.

2/3 WEST RIDING FIELD AMBULANCE.

SHEET 1

NOVEMBER 1918

WAR DIARY
or
INTELLIGENCE SUMMARY.
(Erase heading not required.)

Instructions regarding War Diaries and Intelligence Summaries are contained in F. S. Regs., Part II. and the Staff Manual respectively. Title pages will be prepared in manuscript.

Place	Date	Hour	Summary of Events and Information	Remarks and references to Appendices
CARNIERES	1/11/18		ADMS 62 Division visited the Corps Rest Station.	W.S.
"	2/11/18		The Corps Rest Station was handed over to 7 Field Ambulance. 1 N.C.O and 9 men were attached to each regimental medical officer of 186 Brigade. A working party of 1 N.C.O and 20 men was sent to No 4 C.C.S at Solesmes	W.S.
			The unit proceeded to SOLESMES	W.S.
SOLESMES.	3/11/18		Nothing to report.	W.S.
"	4/11/18		Nothing to report.	W.S.
	5/11/18		The unit moved to ESCARMAIN via VERTAIN and billets in the day to RUESNES	W.S.
RUESNES.	6/11/18		Nothing to report.	W.S.
	7/11/18		The unit moved to ORSINVAL.	W.S.
ORSINVAL	8/11/18		The unit moved to huts at GOMMEGNIES.	W.S.
GOMMEGNIES	9/11/18		Took over the Divisional Rest Station from 2/1 W.R.F.A.	W.S.
GOMMEGNIES	10/11/18		Divisional Rest Station closed and the unit moved to billets at QUÈNE LOUP.	W.S.
QUÈNE LOUP	11/11/18		Moved to the HOSPICE SOUS LE BOIS	W.S.
	12/11/18		Nothing to report.	W.S.

Army Form C. 2118.

SHEET ii

2/3 West Riding Field Ambulance
November 1918

WAR DIARY
or
INTELLIGENCE SUMMARY.
(Erase heading not required.)

Instructions regarding War Diaries and Intelligence Summaries are contained in F.S. Regs., Part II. and the Staff Manual respectively. Title pages will be prepared in manuscript.

Place	Date	Hour	Summary of Events and Information	Remarks and references to Appendices
Sousle Bois	13/11/18		Nothing to report	W.S.
"	14/11/18		"	W.S.
"	15/11/18		"	PJW
"	16/11/18		"	PJW
"	17/11/18		"	PJW
"	18/11/18		The unit moved under the orders of 187 Inf Brigade to OSTERGNIES. The 2/3 W.R.F. Ambulance was responsible for the evacuation of all personnel sick for which purpose 4 M.A.C. cars were attached.	PJW
Ostergnies	19/11/18		Moved via COURCELET and COUSOLRE to MONTIGNIES St CHRISTOPHE.	PJW
Montignies	20/11/18		Moved via HEER-st-FOSTEAU, RAGNIES to GOZÉE.	PJW
Gozée	21/11/18		1 NCO 12 OR. 3 Daimler cars with dressings and medical comforts were sent to report to O.C. Mobile Medical Unit via COLFA.	PJW
	22/11/18		Nothing to report	PJW
	23/11/18		Nothing to report.	PJW
	24/11/18		Moved via MARBAIX and HAM-sur-HEURE to JONCRET	PJW
Joncret	25/11/18		Moved via ACOZ, GOUGNIES, BIESME to METTET.	PJW

Army Form C. 2118.

WAR DIARY
or
INTELLIGENCE SUMMARY. /3 West Riding Field Ambulance

SHEET 1(ii)
NOVEMBER 1918

(Erase heading not required.)

Place	Date	Hour	Summary of Events and Information	Remarks and references to Appendices
METTET	26/11/18		Moved via GRAUX and BIOUL to WARNANT.	
WARNANT	27/11/18		Moved via ANHEE, BOUVIGNES and DINANT to SORINNES	
SORINNES	28/11/18		Nothing to report.	
"	29/11/18		CAPTAIN J.M. PRINGLE M.C. with 8.O.R. R.A.M.C. 1 Sgt 2 O.R. A.S.M.T. and three cars reported to O.C. IX Corps Mobile Midwives unit. Three cars and 12 O.R. R.A.M.C. returned from VIERVES hospital midwives unit.	
"	30/11/18		Nothing to report.	

G.J.Wilmot
LIEUT. COLONEL R.A.M.C.
COMMDG. /3 W.R. (WEST RIDING) FIELD AMBULANCE

MEDICAL

CONFIDENTIAL
Day 1
ORIGINAL COPY

98/24
140/3485

WAR DIARY

OF

2/3rd WEST RIDING FIELD AMBULANCE

From 1.12.1918   To 31.12.1918

VOLUME XXIV

COMMITTEE FOR THE
MEDICAL HISTORY OF THE WAR
6 MAR 1919
Date

MEDICAL

Army Form C. 2118.

2/3 WEST RIDING FIELD AMBULANCE
DECEMBER 1918.
SHEET 1.

WAR DIARY
or
INTELLIGENCE SUMMARY.
(Erase heading not required.)

Instructions regarding War Diaries and Intelligence Summaries are contained in F. S. Regs., Part II. and the Staff Manual respectively. Title pages will be prepared in manuscript.

ORIGINAL

Place	Date	Hour	Summary of Events and Information	Remarks and references to Appendices
SORINNES	1/12/18		Nothing to report	OfW
"	2/12/18		Nothing to report	OfW
"	3/12/18		Nothing to report	OfW
"	4/12/18		Nothing to report	OfW
"	5/12/18		Nothing to report	W.T.
"	6/12/18		Nothing to report	W.T.
"	7/12/18		Nothing to report	W.T.
"	8/12/18		Nothing to report	W.T.
"	9/12/18		Nothing to report	W.T.
AUWEZ	10/12/18		The unit moved under the orders of 187 Inf Brigade to AUWEZ	W.T.
"	11/12/18		The unit moved from AUWEZ to MEAN	W.T.
MEAN	12/12/18		Moved from MEAN to HIMBE	W.T.
HIMBE	13/12/18		Moved from HIMBE to MY	W.T.
MY	14/12/18		Moved from MY to HAUTE BODEUX	W.T.
HAUTE BODEUX	15/12/18		A collecting post for divisional sick was established at TROIS PONTS	W.T.
"	16/12/18		Moved to STAVELOT	W.T.

Army Form C. 2118.

WAR DIARY
or
INTELLIGENCE SUMMARY.
(Erase heading not required.)

2/3 WEST RIDING FIELD AMBULANCE

DECEMBER 1918   SHEET II

Place	Date	Hour	Summary of Events and Information	Remarks and references to Appendices
STAVELOT	17/12/18		Moved via MALMÉDY to NEYWERTZ	WP.
WEYWERTZ	18/12/18		Major J. D. FIDDES R.A.M.C. T.F. assumed command of the Unit.	101
	19/12/18		Capt. H.W. FEATHERSTONE R.A.M.C. S.R. proceeded to England for Demobilisation.	102
	19/12/18		Capt. R.L. Lyn Jones R.A.M.C. T.C. reported for duty & taken on the strength of	102
	20/12/18		Nothing to Report.	102
MONTJOIE	21/12/18		Unit moved & ante march to MONTJOIE.	102
	22/12/18		Major SNEDDON. W. R.A.M.C. (T.F.) proceeded to England. & War Office order.	102
SCHÖNE-SEIFFEN	23/12/18		Unit moved & route march to SCHÖNE-SEIFFEN.	102
HERGARTEN	23/12/18		Unit moved & route march to HERGARTEN.	102
	24/12/18		Nothing to report.	102
	25/12/18		Nothing to report.	102
	26/12/18		Nothing to report.	102
	27/12/18		Nothing to report.	102
	28/12/18		H.Q. & Sanitary section moved to SCHLEIDEN, and no longer attached to this unit.	102
	29/12/18		Nothing to report.	102
	30/12/18		Nothing to report.	102
	31/12/18		Lieut. S.E. MURRAY attached H.Q. w. Rid. Reg. & strength of Group.	102

W Fiddes M. Wh ??

"MEDICAL"

ORIGINAL

62 DIV W.R. 25
Box 2954 140/3490

CONFIDENTIAL

WAR DIARY

of

2/3rd WEST RIDING FIELD AMBULANCE

From January 1st 1919 to January 31st 1919

VOLUME XXV

COMMITTEE FOR THE
MEDICAL HISTORY OF THE WAR
10 MAR. 1919

MEDICAL

Army Form C. 2118.

WAR DIARY
or
INTELLIGENCE SUMMARY
(Erase heading not required.)

2/3 West Riding Field Ambulance
January 1919. Sheet 1.

Place	Date	Hour	Summary of Events and Information	Remarks and references to Appendices
HERBARTEN.	1/1/19		Nothing to report.	JMF
	2/1/19		Nothing to report.	JMF
	3/1/19		Nothing to report.	JMF
	4/1/19		1 O.R. evacuated to CCS (sick).	JMF
	5/1/19		Nothing to report	JMF
	6/1/19		Nothing to report.	JMF
	7/1/19		Capt. D.B. DAVIDSON & 9 O.R. left at 10.30 for Cologne to proceed to GERMANY.	JMF
	8/1/19		Class in First Aid & Hygiene started for B.Coy. as part of Educational Training.	JMF
	9/1/19		Nothing to report	JMF
	10/1/19		Nothing to report	JMF
	11/1/19		Nothing to report	JMF
	12/1/19		Nothing to report	JMF
	13/1/19		Class in First Aid & Hygiene finished. Students returned to units.	JMF
	14/1/19		1 O.R. evacuated to C.C.S. sick.	JMF
	15/1/19		Nothing to report	JMF
	16/1/19		S.G.R. from leave to Cologne for 48 hrs. (187 ODS order SE 24 GS)	Nichols Lt Col

T2134. Wt. W708-776. 500000. 4/15. Sir J. C. & S.

WAR DIARY
or
INTELLIGENCE SUMMARY.
(Erase heading not required.)

Army Form C. 2118.

2/3 West Riding Field Amb 2nd Sheet
January 1915.

Instructions regarding War Diaries and Intelligence Summaries are contained in F. S. Regs., Part II. and the Staff Manual respectively. Title pages will be prepared in manuscript.

Place	Date	Hour	Summary of Events and Information	Remarks and references to Appendices
HERSARTEM.	17/1/15		Nothing to report.	gnt
	18/1/15		Nothing to report.	gnt
	19/1/15		Nothing to report.	gnt
	20/1/15		5 OR proceeded to Cologne on 48 hrs leave	gnt
	21/1/15		Nothing to report.	gnt
	22/1/15		Lieut. A.G. ROGERS, M.O.R.C. (U.S.A.) transferred to 312th Bde R.F.A. as M.O./o.	gnt
	23/1/15		Capt. R.B. ANDERSON, R.C. R.A.M.C. (T) joined the unit & taken on the strength -	gnt
	24/1/15		Capt. H.G. DODD R.A.M.C. (T) joined the unit & taken on the strength	gnt
	25/1/15		Capt. G.J. HAMLEY R.A.M.C. (T.C) joined the unit & taken on the strength.	gnt
	26/1/15		Nothing to report.	gnt
	27/1/15		Nothing to report.	gnt
	28/1/15		Capt. J. MACKENZIE R.A.M.C. (T.C) joined the unit & taken on the strength	gnt
	29/1/15		Nothing to report.	gnt
	30/1/15		Nothing to report.	gnt
	29/1/15		Nothing to report.	gnt
	30/1/15		Nothing to report.	gnt
	31/1/15		Capt. H.G. DODD R.A.M.C. (T) transferred to 5th D of Wellingtons Regt & struck off the strength -	gnt MOfields H.W.

Medical

W 26

CONFIDENTIAL

ORIGINAL WAR DIARY

OF

2/3rd WEST RIDING FIELD AMBULANCE

From 1st February 1919 to 28th February 1919

VOLUME XXVI

Medical

Army Form C. 2118.

WAR DIARY
or
INTELLIGENCE SUMMARY.
(Erase heading not required.)

2/3 West Riding Field Ambulance

Feb. 1919   1st Sheet

Place	Date	Hour	Summary of Events and Information	Remarks and references to Appendices
Hergarten	1.2.19		Lt Col Riddle MC. Officers proceeded to U.K. on leave.	gmg
	2.2.19		Sent Sendin classes compiled — Initiated Pte Dunnicliffe H. Rennie G. Kelly. to Report.	gmg
	3.2.19		Capt 2nd McKenzie Rennie detailed for duty at Kreuzkap.	gmg
	4.2.19		do.	
	5.2.19		do.	gmg
	6.2.19		do.	gmg
	7.2.19		S.O.R. proceeded on 48 hours leave to Cologne. Capt & J/S Davidson returned from Berlin.	gmg
	8.2.19		Nothing to Report	gmg
	9.2.19		nothing to Report	gmg
	10.2.19		nothing to Report	gmg
	11.2.19		nothing to Report	gmg
	12.2.19		nothing to Report	gmg
	13.2.19		G.O.R. returned from Germany.	gmg
	14.2.19		Lt. O. R. Miller from Germany — White & Park now Cook. Lectures to unit by G.P.M.S.	gmg
	15.2.19		nothing to Report	
	16.2.19		Captain D.A. Davidson Rennie left unit for demobilisation in U.K.	gmg
	17.2.19		Lecture welcoming by Bishop Arthram on Germany attended by O.R.	gmg
	18.2.19		Lecture Swiss on Rennie Duncan.	gmg

T2134. Wt. W708—776. 500000. 4/15. Sir J.C.&S.

Army Form C. 2118.

2/3 West Riding Field Ambulance
Feb 1919. 2nd Sheet.

WAR DIARY
or
INTELLIGENCE SUMMARY.
(Erase heading not required.)

Place	Date	Hour	Summary of Events and Information	Remarks and references to Appendices
HERGARTEN. Germany.	19/2/15		Lt Col. J D FIDDES assumed cmd from Capt a Topp amoured	
	20/2/15		Nothing to report	
	21/2/19		Nothing to report	
	22/2/15		7 O.R. proceed to Cologne on 48 hrs leave.	
	23/2/15		25 OR inoculated against Typhoid & Paratyphoid fevers	
	24/2/15		Nothing to report	
	25/2/15		40 OR inoculated against Typhoid & Paratyphoid fevers	
	26/2/15		Nothing to report	
	27/2/15		21 OR inoculated against Typhoid & Paratyphoid fevers	
	28/2/15		Capt HANLEY R.ume. L.F. a 2/M Brown R.A.M.C. proceed on 14 days leave to U.K.	

CONFIDENTIAL
Mar 1919

ORIGINAL
WAR DIARY
OF
2/3rd WEST RIDING FIELD AMBULANCE

From 1st March 1919 To 31st March 1919

VOLUME XXVII

Medical

WAR DIARY
or
INTELLIGENCE SUMMARY
(Erase heading not required.)

Army Form C. 2118.

2/3 West Riding Field Ambulance
1st Sheet.

Place	Date	Hour	Summary of Events and Information	Remarks and references to Appendices
BERGHEIM Germany	1/3/45		Nothing to report	JAZ
	2/3/45		Nothing to report	JAZ
	3/3/45		Nothing to report	JAZ
	4/3/45		Capt S.J. McDONALD RAMC (TC) attached for duty from 2/2 West Riding Fd Amb	JAZ
	5/3/45		Capt DONALD RAMC(TC) left with advance party for GIRBELSRATH	JAZ
	6/3/45		Transport & unit moved off to DUREN at 0900 hrs	JAZ
			Unit left for GIRBELSRATH at 0530 hrs arrived complete 1300 hrs	JAZ
GIRBELSRATH Germany	7/3/45		Settling in report	JAZ
	8/3/45		Nothing to report	JAZ
	9/3/45		Nothing to report	JAZ
	10/3/45		Nothing to report	JAZ
	11/3/45		Nothing to report	JAZ
	12/3/45		Capt J.O. Green reported for duty from 6th Ous.	JAZ
	13/3/45		Major J.R. Black's return in 14 days leave to UK.	JAZ
	14/3/45		Nothing to report	JAZ
	15/3/45		Lt/Col 2nd Service returned from leave in UK.	JAZ
	16/3/45		Nothing to report	JStocking Lt.Col
	17/3/45		Nothing to report	

WAR DIARY
or
INTELLIGENCE SUMMARY.
(Erase heading not required.)

2/3 West Riding Fd Amb
2nd Sheet

Place	Date	Hour	Summary of Events and Information	Remarks and references to Appendices
ARBEISRATH Germany	17/3/19		Orders received for A/Lt Col. J.D. FIDDES R.A.M.C (T.F) to proceed to England to demobilize J.Z.	
	18/3/19		A/Lt Col J.D. FIDDES proceeded to England for Demobilisation. Capt A/W. Donald took over temporary command of this unit.	
	19/3/19		Capt J. McKenzie R.A.M.C. reported from detached duty at Malmedy	
	20/3/19		Capt J. McKenzie R.A.M.C. proceeded to Dispersal Station, DÜREN for demobilisation.	
	21/3/19		Nothing to report	
	22/3/19		Nothing to report	
	23/3/19		Capt 2/J Hanley R.A.M.C. returned off leave of absence to U.K.	
	24/3/19		Nothing to report	
	25/3/19		Nothing to report	
	26/3/19		Nothing to report	
	27/3/19		Capt 2/O Grane R.A.M.C proceeded as M O i/c 9th Batt Seaforth Highlanders.	
	28/3/19		Nothing to report	
	29/3/19		Nothing to report	
	29/3/19		Nothing to report	
	30/3/19		Major J M PRINGLE R.A.M.C (T.F) returned off leave of absence to U.K.	
	31/3/19		Major J M PRINGLE R.A.M.C (T.F) took over command of unit.	

Medical

ORIGINAL

WAR DIARY

OF

2/3RD WEST RIDING FIELD AMBULANCE

FROM 1ST APRIL 1919 TO 30TH APRIL 1919

VOLUME XXVIII

April 1919
CONFIDENTIAL

Medical

WAR DIARY
~~INTELLIGENCE~~ SUMMARY.
(Erase heading not required.)

Army Form C. 2118.

3rd Fd Amb First Australian
1st Sheet

Place	Date	Hour	Summary of Events and Information	Remarks and references to Appendices
Swielneh	1.4.19		Nothing to report	
	2.4.19		Nothing to report	
	3.4.19		Nothing to report	
	4.4.19		Nothing to report	
	5.4.19		Nothing to report	
Surafend	6.4.19		Capt G. J. Stanley reported for duty 6.15 a.p.g. 20 and Bethlehem duplets arrived	
Surafend	7.4.19		Nothing to report	
Surafend	8.4.19		Nothing to report	
do	9.4.19		Nothing to report	
do	10.4.19		Nothing to report	
do	11.4.19		Nothing to report	
do	12.4.19		Nothing to report	
do	13.4.19		Nothing to report	
do	14.4.19		Nothing to report	
do	15.4.19		Nothing to report	
do	16.4.19		Nothing to report	
do	17.4.19		Nothing to report	

… Army Form C. 2118.

WAR DIARY
or
INTELLIGENCE SUMMARY.
(Erase heading not required.)

1/3rd West Riding Field Ambulance
2nd Sheet

Place	Date	Hour	Summary of Events and Information	Remarks and references to Appendices
Fauquembergues	18 Aug 16	6 pm	Lieut Colonel P.J. Rutherford Received found unit and assumed command on from the 17th Inst.	
"	19		Routine	P.R
"	20			P.R
"	21			P.R
"	22			P.R
"	23		attached J.M.S. employment at Colembert	P.R
"	24		First Bowie reported for duty. Captain Donald left unit to duty as A/DADMS	P.R
"	25			P.R
"	26		Routine	P.R
"	27			P.R
"	28			P.R
"	29		Lieu (2D) Reinforcement arrived includes 1 Sergt 1 Corp 2 Lance Corporals & 6 Privates	P.R
"	30		Other - 1 Private in P/11 Ord Recd Field held for Inspection of Reinforcements by ADMS & DADMS visited Field Ambulance - Unit had sports on the afternoon	P.R

Seven Rutherford
Lieut Colonel
1/3rd West Riding Field Ambulance

Medical

ORIGINAL
May 1919

CONFIDENTIAL

War Diary

of

2/3 West Riding Field Amb

From May 1st 1919 to May 31st 1919

Volume XXIX

Medical

Army Form C. 2118.

WAR DIARY
or
INTELLIGENCE SUMMARY
(Erase heading not required.)

2/3 WEST RIDING FIELD AMBULANCE
LIEUT COLONEL P T RUTHERFORD
RAMC TF

Place	Date	Hour	Summary of Events and Information	Remarks and references to Appendices
GIRBIGSRATH	1-5-19	6/an	Visited BERG-STEIN, no possibility of billeting for scarcely found the available depôts and Bergheim	OLP
"	2-5-19	-	Conference at ADMS Office KREUZAU. Reinforcement - for Rhine-army - about 3 3 men from CCS to Division Hospital R	OCR
"	3-5-19	-	Visited MANBACH & BIRK - both village satisfactory for billeting troops - water supply poor - Field San.	OLR
"	4-5-19	-	Routine - Report in village. 1 MANBACH & BIRCH sent to 3 Sth West Brigade	OCR
"	5-5-19	-	Routine. Bill Tents as have put up in Recreation field in order to augment hospital	OCR
			Accommodation	
"	6-5-19	-	Routine. Strong TF Officers 4. OR. 137.	
	7		Routine	
	8		Routine	
	9		Inspection of Unit by Lieut General Sir A J GODLEY KCB KCMG Commanding IV Corps. Accompanied by DDMS IV Corps. and ADMS Anglesea Division	
	10		Meeting at 64 CCS called by DMS Army John Rhine	
	11		Routine	
	12		Routine	
	13		Routine	
	14		Routine	

2/3RD
WEST RIDING
FIELD AMBULANCE

Army Form C. 2118.

WAR DIARY
or
INTELLIGENCE SUMMARY.
(Erase heading not required.)

2/3 WEST RIDING FIELD AMBULANCE
by LIEUT COL P.T. RUTHERFORD

Instructions regarding War Diaries and Intelligence Summaries are contained in F.S. Regs., Part II. and the Staff Manual respectively. Title pages will be prepared in manuscript.

Place	Date	Hour	Summary of Events and Information	Remarks and references to Appendices
GIRBLESRATH	15-5-19	6 pm	Routine	
"	16-5-19	6 pm	33 OR reported from 1/4 Seaforth Highlanders for attachment.	
"	17-5-19	6 pm	Routine. Preliminary training further personnel commenced.	
"	18-5-19	6 pm	10 OR from 8th Black Watch attached for attachment to transport. (H.T.)	
"	19-5-19	6 pm	from 1/4 Gordons and 53rd Gordons reporting attachment	
"	20-5-19	6 pm	3 OR from 53rd Gordons reported for attachment – detail as attached	
"			Personnel on Manoeuvre Discharge – Routine	
"	21-5-19	6 pm		
"	22-5-19	6 pm	Conference at ADMS office. Unit put in 4 hour notice to move. Have under orders of 2 SK Lower Rifle	
DAREN	23-5-19	6 pm	This Unit took over hospital at BEHRER SEMINAR at 15.00 hours from 2/2 West Riding Field Ambulance	
"	24-5-19	6 pm	Routine. Clearin of hospital & rounds, rearranging wards.	
"	25-5-19	6 pm	DMS British Army of Rhine, DDMS IV Corps Visited and inspected hospital	
"	26-5-19	6 pm	ADMS Visited hospital	
"	27-5-19	6 pm	} Routine	
"	28-5-19	6 pm		
"	29-5-19	6 pm		
"	30-5-19	6 pm		
"	31-5-19	6 pm		

Lucind Rutherford
Lieut Colonel
2/3rd West Riding Field Ambulance

ORIGINAL

WAR DIARY (MEDICAL)

OF

2/3RD WEST RIDING FIELD AMBULANCE

From 1/6/1919 to 30/6/1919

VOLUME XXX

Army Form C. 2118.

MEDICAL

WAR DIARY
or
INTELLIGENCE SUMMARY.

2/3 WEST RIDING FIELD AMBULANCE
by
LIEUT COLONEL P.T. RUTHERFORD RAMC

SHEET 1

(Erase heading not required.)

Place	Date	Hour	Summary of Events and Information	Remarks and references to Appendices
DÜREN	1-6-19	6pm	Routine	
	2-6-19		Attended DMS Conference - Visited 04416 with ADMS establishing the field	
			Ambulance would move on to that assumption of hostilities.	
	3-6-19		Routine and Training of attached personnel	
	4-6-19		"	
	5-6-19		"	
	7-6-19		"	
	8-6-19		"	
	9-6-19		"	
	10-6-19		"	
	11-6-19		"	
	12-6-19		"	
	13-6-19		"	
	14-6-19		"	
	15-6-19		DDMS Iv Corps and Colonel Bliss AMS visited Hospital	
	16-6-19		Routine	

MEDICAL

Army Form C. 2118.

WAR DIARY
or
INTELLIGENCE SUMMARY.
(Erase heading not required.)

2/3rd West Riding Field Ambulance
by
Lieut. Colonel P.T. RUTHERFORD RAMC

Instructions regarding War Diaries and Intelligence Summaries are contained in F. S. Regs., Part II. and the Staff Manual respectively. Title pages will be prepared in manuscript.

SHEET II

Place	Date	Hour	Summary of Events and Information	Remarks and references to Appendices
OHLIGS	17.6.19		J-3 day	
		2400	1 Off 70 OR. entrained at Dürren and arrived at OHLIGS at 17.40 hour.	PJR
			Lieut BOWIE and Capt TQMBrown had left school at Dürren & handing over hospital to incoming Field Ambulance. Rheinland Division. Transport marched Dürren to OHLIGS by road starting at 1400 hour from Billy Royale Transport Rheinish Infant.	PJR
			Summary until 17 hour - journey to OHLIGS took 3 days.	PJR
	18.6.19	2200	Lieut BOWIE & party reported being landed over hospital at DÜRREN to 116" Field Ambulance Rheinland Division at 1700 hour.	PJR
			Arrangements made with OC of 27' Field Ambulance and OC 28' Field Ambulance that one then hospital when they are. 1 Theo & 7 mm can to SOLINGEN a holding park, takes out from 21' Field Ambulance on morning of 19-6-19 (J-1 day).	PJR
			The hospital Sch at SOLINGEN will be used as a Sick Thrombic Collecting and Evacuating Station - from which all can will be sent to OHLIGS	PJR
	19.6.19		J-1 day. Routine.	PJR
	20.6.19		Routine.	PJR
	20.6.19		Routine.	PJR

MEDICAL

WAR DIARY
or
INTELLIGENCE SUMMARY. 2/3wg-1 Riding Field Ambulance
by
SHEET III   LIEUT COLONEL P.T. RUTHERFORD

Army Form C. 2118.

Place	Date	Hour	Summary of Events and Information	Remarks and references to Appendices
OHLIES	22-64	6pm	Service	Cl
	23		Routine	Cl
	24		Routine	Cl
	25		Routine	Cl
	26		Routine	Cl
	27		Routine	Cl
	28		Peace Signed at VERSAILLES	Cl
	29		Routine	Cl
	30		T. A. Day. advance party left OHLIES for Durn at 0700 hours. Take over LEHRER SEMINAR from 16" Field Ambulance Rhineland Division	Cl

Lionel Rutherford Lieut Colonel
2/3rd West Riding Field Ambulance

CONFIDENTIAL

ORIGINAL

WAR DIARY

OF

2/3rd WEST RIDING FIELD AMBULANCE

FROM 1-7-1919 TO 31-7-1919

VOLUME XXXI

July 1919

Army Form C. 2118.

WAR DIARY
or
INTELLIGENCE SUMMARY. 2/3 W.R. RIDING FIELD AMBULANCE
By Thisis Col P.T Rutherford
(Erase heading not required.)

Instructions regarding War Diaries and Intelligence Summaries are contained in F.S. Regs., Part II. and the Staff Manual respectively. Title pages will be prepared in manuscript.

Place	Date	Hour	Summary of Events and Information	Remarks and references to Appendices
OWLES	1/7/19	1800hr	Routine	PK
DUREN	2-7-19	1800	Visit Lt of Officers. Inspected by brd. Personnel by train & motor driven 1800hrs	PK
"	3-7-19	—	Routine	PK
	4-7-19	—	"	PK
	5-7-19	—	"	PK
	6-7-19	—	"	PK
	7-7-19	—	"	PK
	8-7-19	—	Lieut Col P.T Rutherford OBE. S.M. TORR DCM, Sgt Dypument MM, QMS STEAD Pte SCOTT Left DUREN for PARIS	PK
	9-7-19	—	Routine	PK
	10-7-19	—	"	PK
	11-7-19	—	"	PK
	12-7-19	—	"	PK
	13-7-19	—	"	PK
	14-7-19	—	"	PK
	15-7-19	—	"	PK
	16-7-19	—	"	PK

Manual

Army Form C. 2118.

WAR DIARY
or
INTELLIGENCE SUMMARY.   2/3rd Edin Field Ambulance
By Lieut Col DT Rutherford RE

(Erase heading not required.)

Place	Date	Hour	Summary of Events and Information	Remarks and references to Appendices
DAREN	17·7·19	8·00	Routine	PK
"	18·7·19	"	"	CLR
"	19·7·19	"	"	CLR
"	20·7·19	"	"	CLR
"	21·7·19	"	— Attached Infantry Reinforces ↓	CLR
"	22·7·19	"	↓ France.	CLR
"	23·7·19	"	"	CLR
"	24·7·19	"	"	CLR
"	25·7·19	"	"	CLR
"	26·7·19	"	"	CLR
"	27·7·19	"	"	CLR
"	28·7·19	"	"	PM
"	29·7·19	"	"	PK
"	30·7·19	"	"	CLR
"	31·7·19	"	S.M.S Caprera of Donc Ame On the CLOOME	CLR

Sgnd Rutherford
Lieut Colonel - RAMC

2/3rd West Riding Field Ambulance

COMMITTEE FOR THE
JAN 1920
MEDICAL HISTORY OF THE WAR

Medical
Army Form C. 2118.

WAR DIARY
or
INTELLIGENCE SUMMARY.
(Erase heading not required.)

Instructions regarding War Diaries and Intelligence Summaries are contained in F.S. Regs., Part II. and the Staff Manual respectively. Title pages will be prepared in manuscript.

Place	Date	Hour	Summary of Events and Information	Remarks and references to Appendices
Duren	1/8/19	18.00	Routine AMO	
"	2/8/19	"	" AMO	
"	3/8/19	"	" AMO	
"	4/8/19	"	" AMO	
"	5/8/19	"	" AMO	
"	6/8/19	"	" AMO	
"	7/8/19	"	Horses, vehicles withdrawn little loaded in view of move to Great Britain AMO	
"	8/8/19	"	Routine AMO	
"	9/8/19	"	M.T. transport withdrawn & sent to M.T. Bordeaux AMO	
"	10/8/19	"	Routine AMO	
"	11/8/19	"	" AMO	
"	12/8/19	"	" AMO	
"	13/8/19	"	" AMO	
"	14/8/19	18.30	2/Lt Duver at 18.30 & entrained for Calais AMO	
"	15/8/19		En route AMO	
Calais	16/8/19	7.00	Arrived Calais 7.00 hrs 2/Lt Palmer & disembarked. 2/Lt Palmer & embarked at 11.30 hrs Conserdon 1x 40 hrs & disembarked Dover at 15.25 hrs in Victoria arr. Victoria at 18.30 hrs & entrained in London for night AMO unit accommodated in London for night AMO	

Army Form C. 2118.

WAR DIARY
or
INTELLIGENCE SUMMARY.
(Erase heading not required.)

Instructions regarding War Diaries and Intelligence Summaries are contained in F. S. Regs., Part II. and the Staff Manual respectively. Title pages will be prepared in manuscript.

Place	Date	Hour	Summary of Events and Information	Remarks and references to Appendices
London	17/8/19	11.40 hrs	Entrained at King's Cross & R/V at 1140 hrs for Catterick Camp.	Am. Pattern
Catterick Camp	18/8/19	18.00	Camp 21.15 hrs & billeted. AMD	
	19/8/19	18.00	Catterick Camp Routine. AMD	
			"	AMB
"	20/8/19	18.00	Routine. Major A.W. [illeg] M.L. & Lieut. D.S. Bowie proceeded to support A.D.M.S. Highlands	
"	21/8/19	18.00	arrived at Clipstone Camp. AMD	
"			Routine AMD	
"	22/8/19 07.10	Unit entrained Catterick Camp at 07.10 hrs for Clipstone Camp. Arrived Clipstone Camp at 15.00 hrs & billeted. AMD	
Clipstone Camp	23/8/19	18.00	Routine AMD	
"	24/8/19	18.00	" AMD	
"	25/8/19	18.00	" AMD	
"	26/8/19	18.00	Lieut D.S. Bowie proceeded on 15 days leave to Scotland AMD	
"	27/8/19	18.00	Routine AMD	
"	28/8/19	18.00	" AMD	
"	29/8/19	18.00	" AMD	
"	30/8/19	18.00	" AMD	
"	31/8/19	18.00	" AMD	

A. Ambrose Major
a/O.C. 1/s [illeg]

www.ingramcontent.com/pod-product-compliance
Lightning Source LLC
Chambersburg PA
CBHW081405160426
43193CB00013B/2107